SO WHAT ARE YOU ABOUT, THEN, "AGENT GRAVES"?

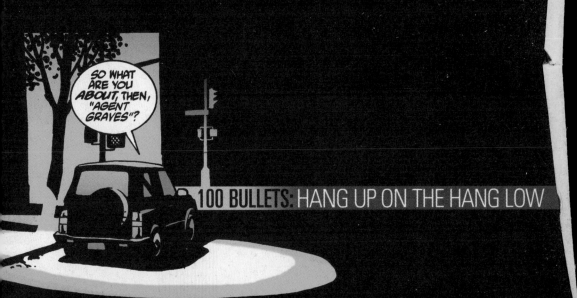

100 BULLETS: HANG UP ON THE HANG LOW

HANG UP ON THE HANG LOW

100 BULLETS:

Brian Azzarello Writer **Eduardo Risso** Artist **Patricia Mulvihill** Colorist **Digital Chameleon** Separator

Clem Robins Letterer **Dave Johnson** Covers 100 BULLETS created by Brian Azzarello and Eduardo Risso

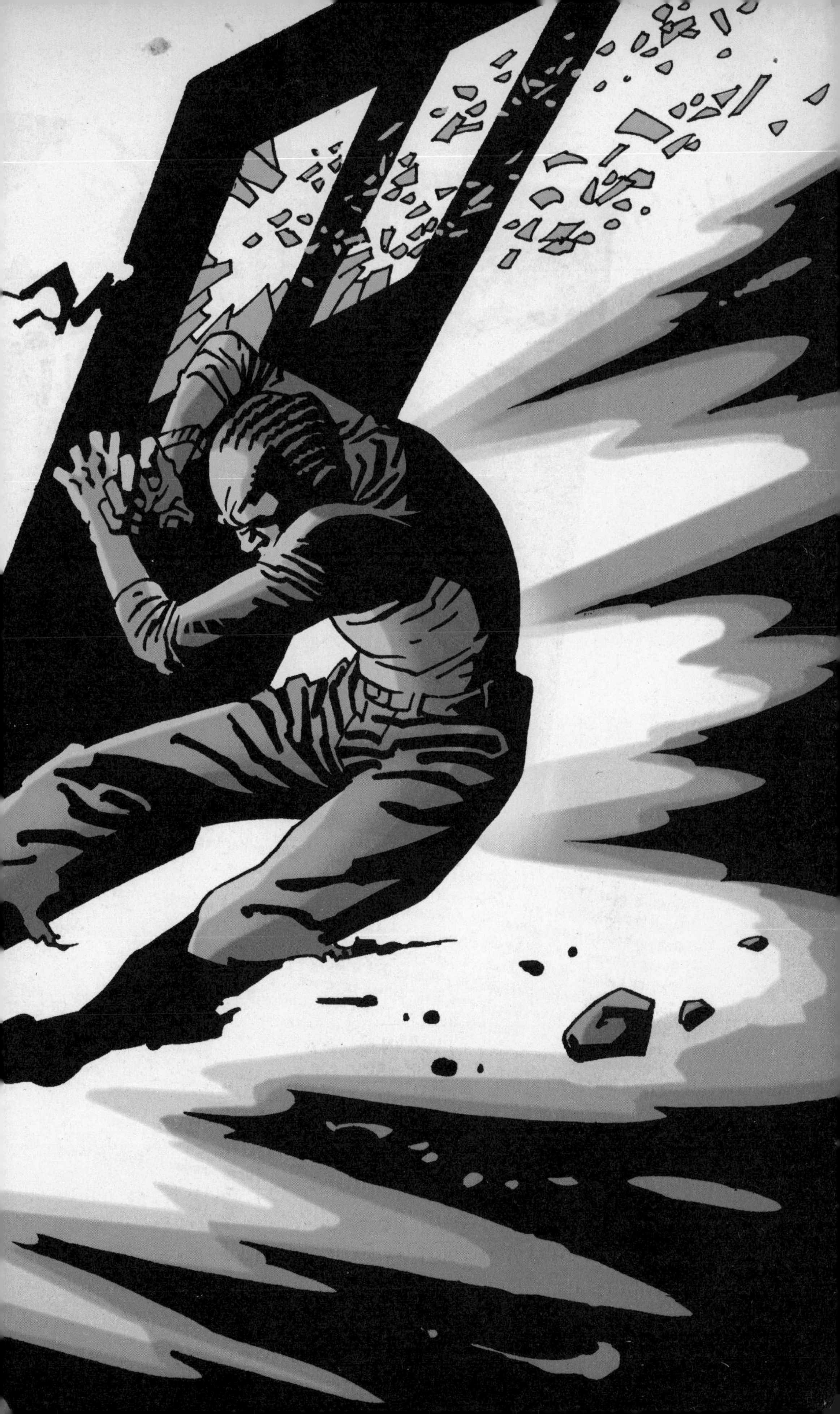

Karen Berger VP-Executive Editor Axel Alonso Editor-original series Jennifer Lee Assistant Editor-original series
Scott Nybakken Editor-collected edition Nick J. Napolitano Associate Editor-collected edition
Robbin Brosterman Senior Art Director Paul Levitz President & Publisher
Georg Brewer VP-Design & Retail Product Development Richard Bruning Senior VP-Creative Director
Patrick Caldon Senior VP-Finance & Operations Chris Caramalis VP-Finance
Terri Cunningham VP-Managing Editor Alison Gill VP-Manufacturing Rich Johnson VP-Book Trade Sales
Hank Kanalz VP-General Manager, WildStorm Lillian Laserson Senior VP & General Counsel
Jim Lee Editorial Director-WildStorm David McKillips VP-Advertising & Custom Publishing
John Nee VP-Business Development Gregory Noveck Senior VP-Creative Affairs
Cheryl Rubin Senior VP-Brand Management Bob Wayne VP-Sales & Marketing

100 BULLETS: HANG UP ON THE HANG LOW Published by DC Comics. Cover and compilation copyright © 2001 DC Comics.
All Rights Reserved. Originally published in single magazine form as 100 BULLETS 15-19. Copyright © 2000, 2001 Brian
Azzarello and DC Comics. All Rights Reserved. All characters, their distinctive likenesses and related elements featured
in this publication are trademarks of DC Comics. The stories, characters, and incidents featured in this publication are
entirely fictional. DC Comics does not read or accept unsolicited submissions of ideas, stories or artwork.
DC Comics, 1700 Broadway, New York, NY 10019. A Warner Bros. Entertainment Company.
Printed in Canada. Third Printing. ISBN: 1-56389-855-1. Cover illustration by Dave Johnson and Eduardo Risso.
Publication design by Louis Prandi.

BAM BAM BAM

INTRODUCTION

Crafted by writer Brian Azzarello and artist Eduardo Risso, 100 BULLETS is arguably the finest collaborative comic book this medium has produced in decades, weaving such themes as fatherhood, baseball and organized crime into a series of poignant tales as dark in their humor as they are gut-wrenching in their pathos.

They are the stories of haunted, marginalized people who slip through life on sheer inertia, until their destinies are irrevocably changed by a man known only as Agent Graves. A cross between the archangel Gabriel and an old-fashioned G-man, the ghostlike Graves comes into their lives with a powerful handgun and 100 untraceable bullets. His offer? *Opportunity*.

The opportunity to exact vengeance — or the opportunity to make amends.

It is the dichotomy between these two choices which makes 100 BULLETS so engaging. While the untraceable bullets offer immunity from the law, the characters find that they cannot shield themselves from the moral consequences of their actions.

In this third collected volume — which features my favorite story arc of the series so far — Agent Graves presents his Faustian bargain to Louis Hughes, a.k.a. Loop. As a young black man coming of age in urban Philadelphia, Loop isn't a gangbanger. At least not yet. But he does have a chip on his shoulder about his absentee father — a father he both resents and yearns for at the same time. Fate has it that Curtis Hughes, Loop's father, is as rudderless as his son, wasting his days away collecting debts for a creepy Mister Magoo loanshark — until the day Graves appears.

With stark, dead-on dialogue punctuating smooth, stylized artwork, Azzarello and Risso bring father and son together in a combustive story about second chances in the City of Brotherly Love.

As Agent Graves says, it's not how it got started that matters, it's how it ends.

So start reading. Opportunity awaits!

— Jim Lee

One of contemporary comics' most popular creators, Jim Lee has been writing and drawing in the medium for almost fifteen years. Along the way, he co-founded Image Comics, created WildStorm Productions, and transformed himself into a Vegas-grade card shark.

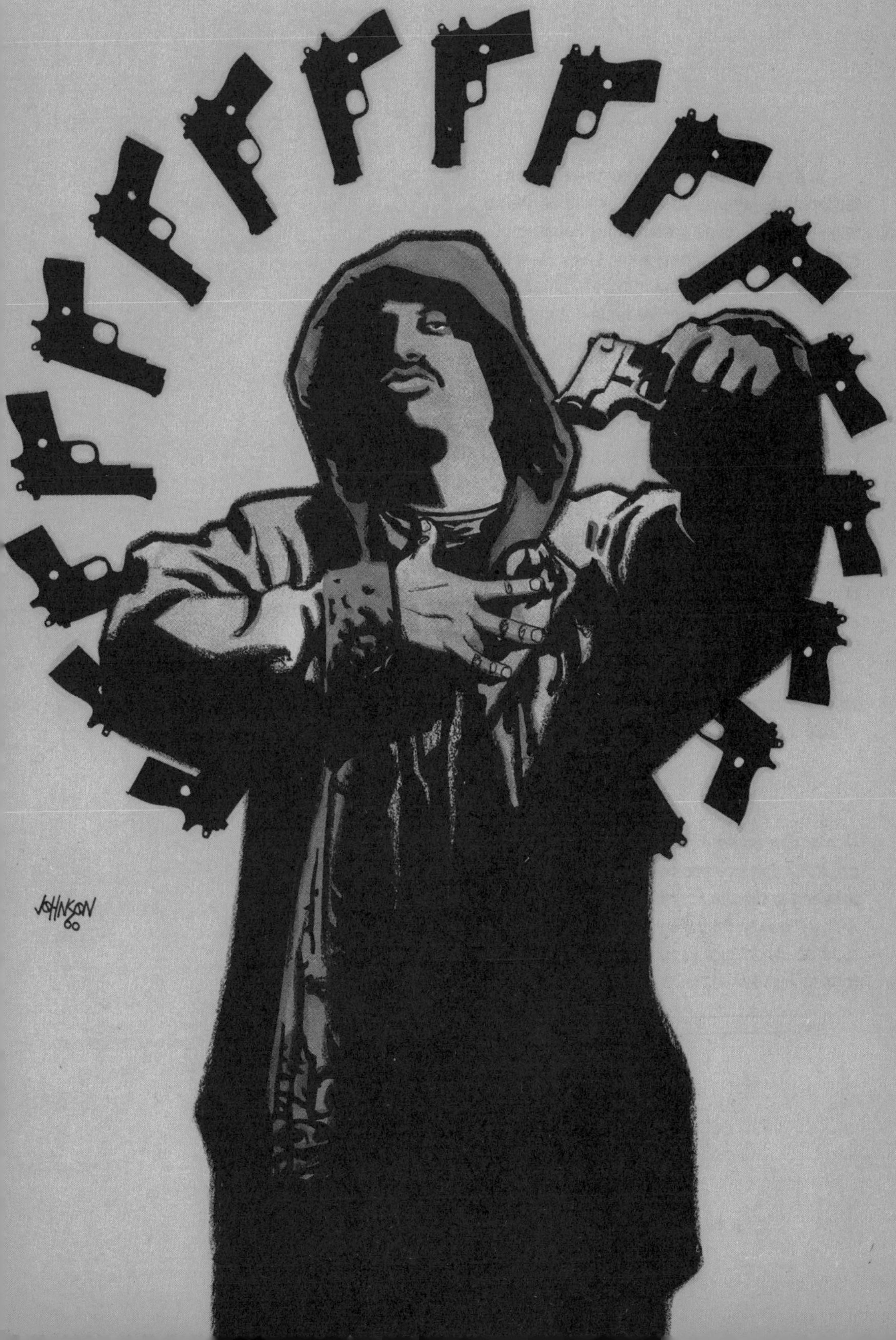
JOHNSON
06

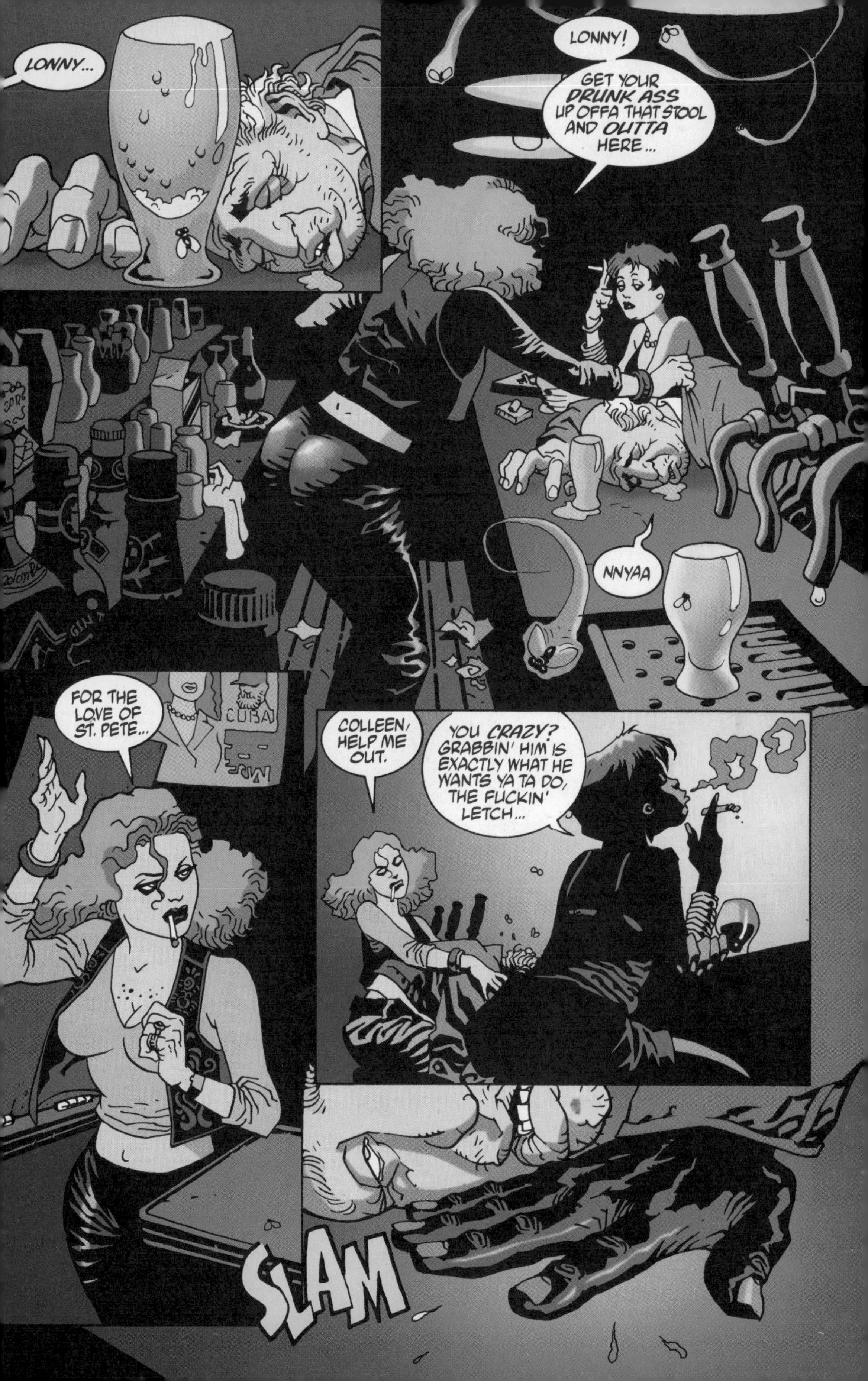
LONNY...
LONNY!
GET YOUR DRUNK ASS UP OFFA THAT STOOL AND OUTTA HERE...
NNYAA
FOR THE LOVE OF ST. PETE...
COLLEEN, HELP ME OUT.
YOU CRAZY? GRABBIN' HIM IS EXACTLY WHAT HE WANTS YA TA DO, THE FUCKIN' LETCH...
SLAM

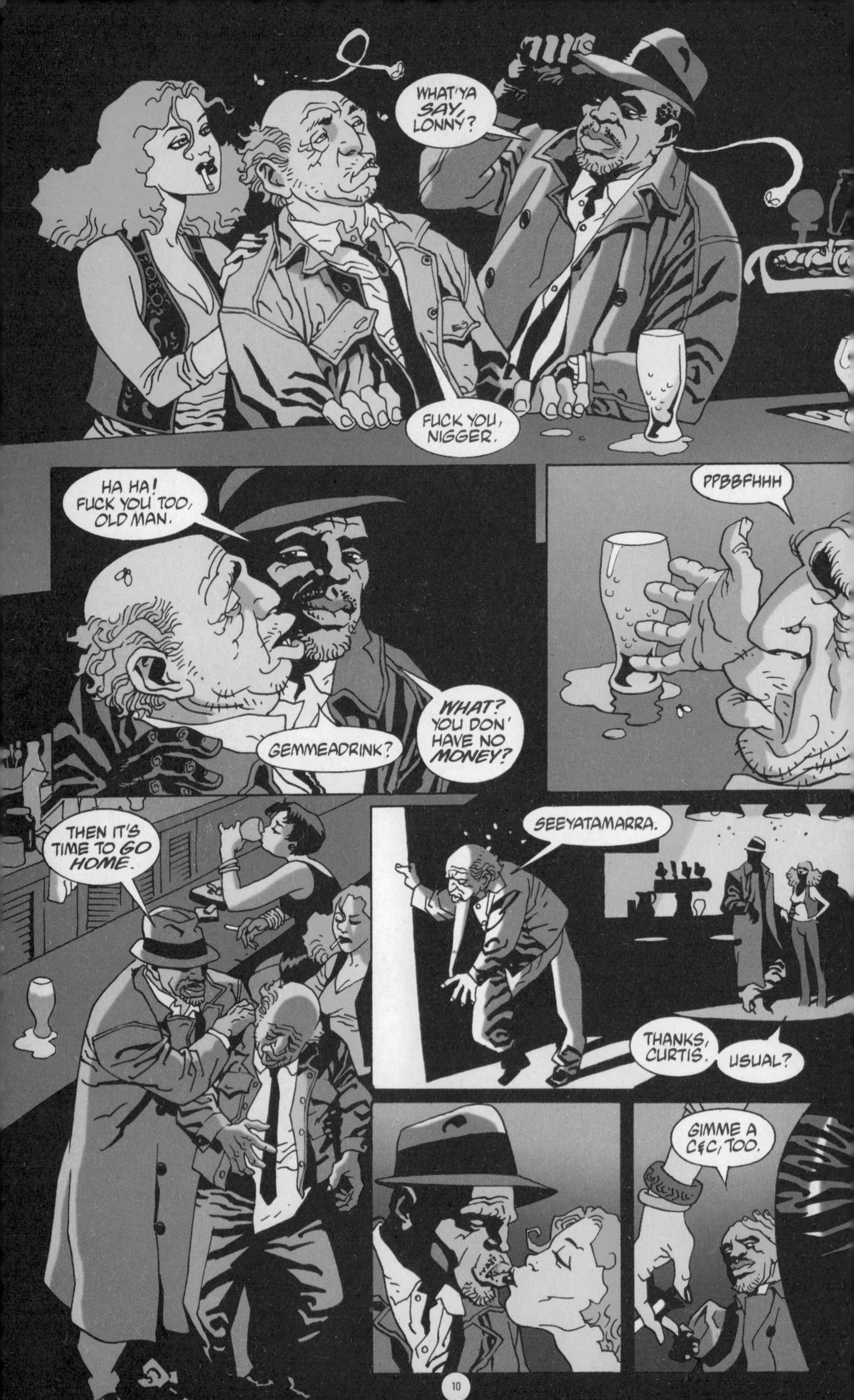
WHAT'YA SAY, LONNY?
FUCK YOU, NIGGER.
HA HA! FUCK YOU TOO, OLD MAN.
GEMMEADRINK?
WHAT? YOU DON' HAVE NO MONEY?
PPBBFHHH
THEN IT'S TIME TO GO HOME.
SEEYATAMARRA.
THANKS, CURTIS.
USUAL?
GIMME A C&C, TOO.

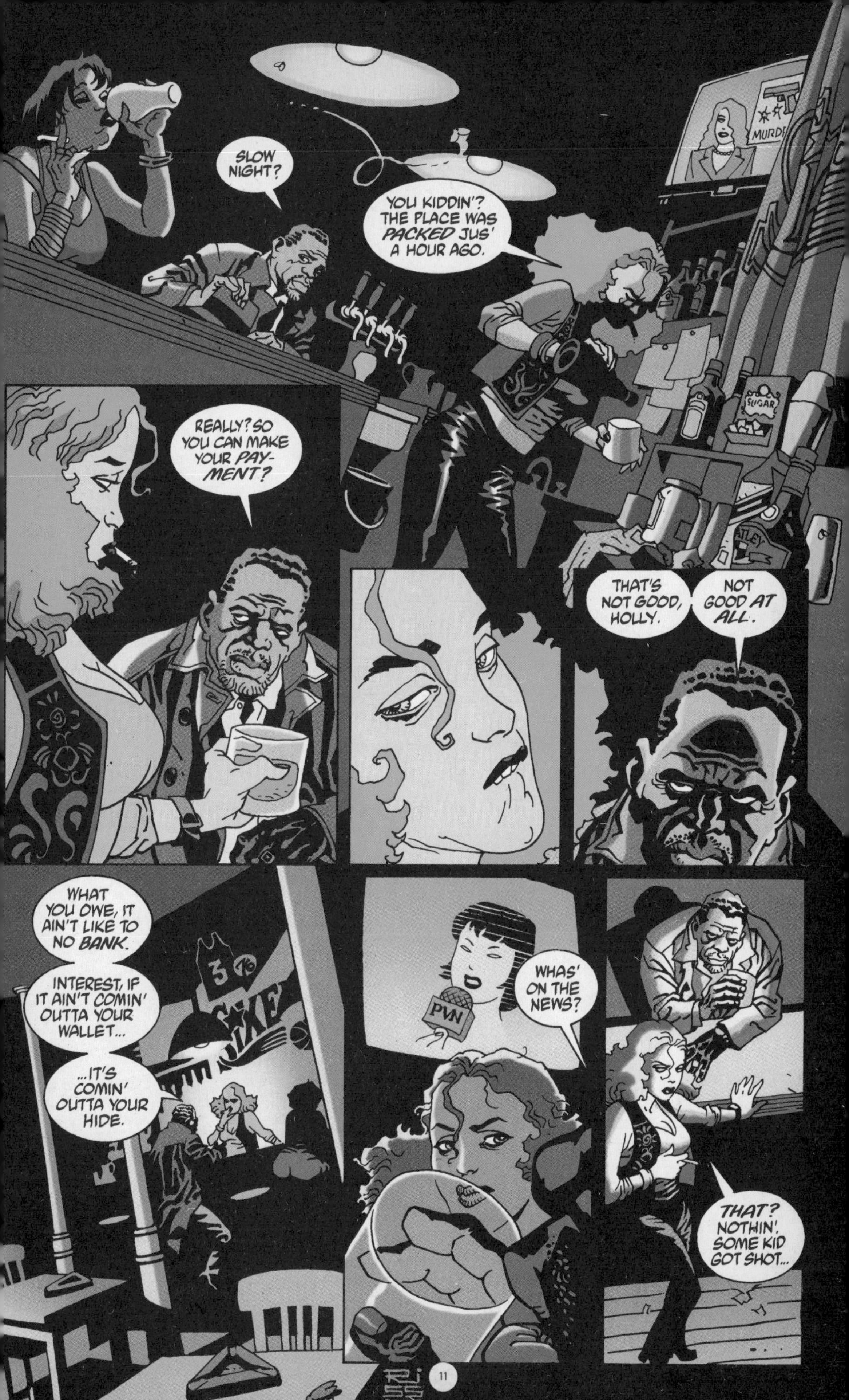

SLOW NIGHT?
YOU KIDDIN'? THE PLACE WAS PACKED JUS' A HOUR AGO.
REALLY? SO YOU CAN MAKE YOUR PAY-MENT?
THAT'S NOT GOOD, HOLLY.
NOT GOOD AT ALL.
WHAT YOU OWE, IT AIN'T LIKE TO NO BANK.
INTEREST, IF IT AIN'T COMIN' OUTTA YOUR WALLET...
...IT'S COMIN' OUTTA YOUR HIDE.
PVN
WHAS' ON THE NEWS?
THAT? NOTHIN'. SOME KID GOT SHOT...

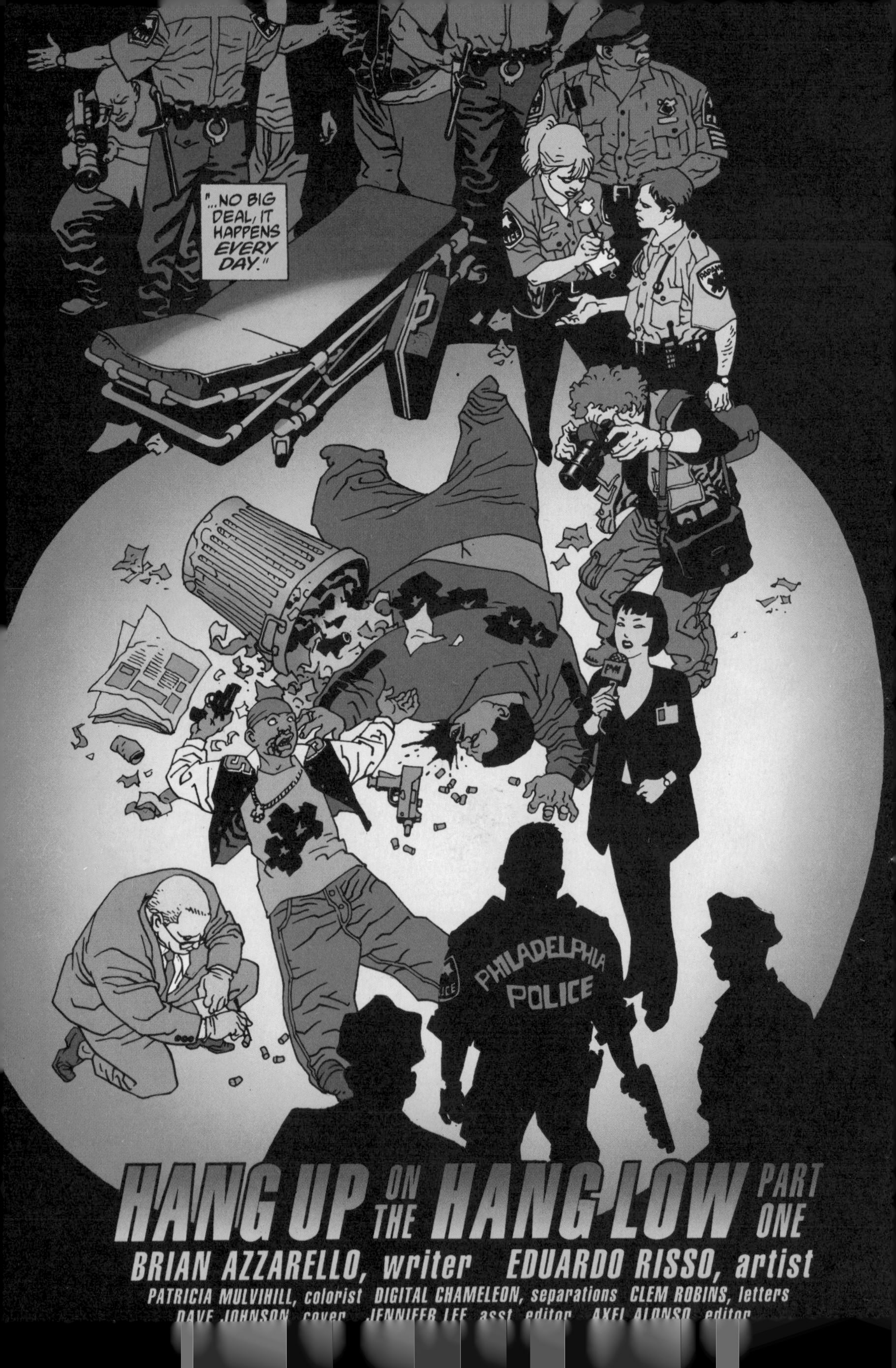
"...NO BIG DEAL, IT HAPPENS EVERY DAY."
PHILADELPHIA POLICE
POLICE
HANG UP ON THE HANG LOW PART ONE
BRIAN AZZARELLO, writer EDUARDO RISSO, artist
PATRICIA MULVIHILL, colorist DIGITAL CHAMELEON, separations CLEM ROBINS, letters
DAVE JOHNSON, cover JENNIFER LEE, asst. editor AXEL ALONSO, editor

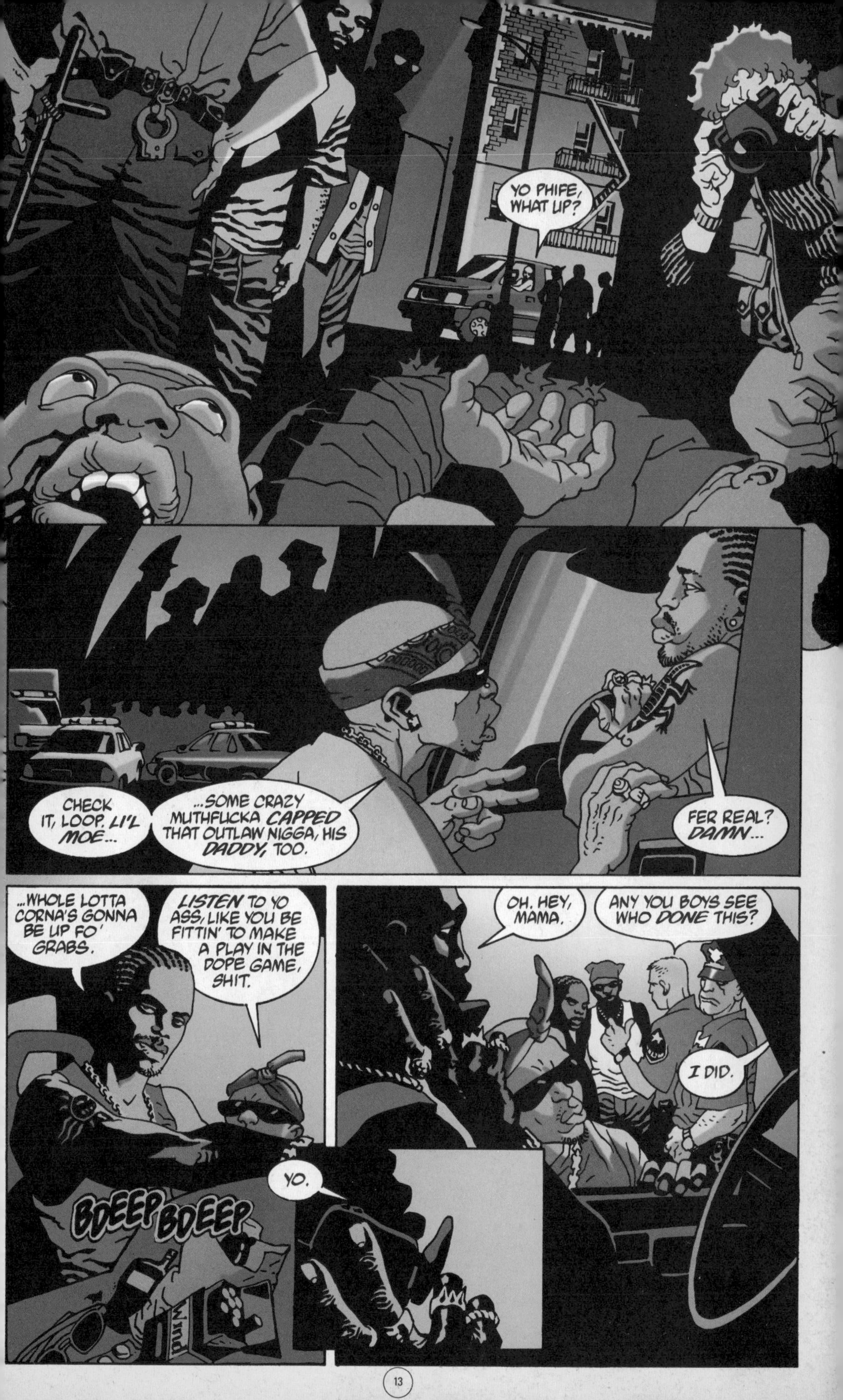
YO PHIFE, WHAT UP?
CHECK IT, LOOP. LI'L MOE...
...SOME CRAZY MUTHFUCKA CAPPED THAT OUTLAW NIGGA, HIS DADDY, TOO.
FER REAL? DAMN...
...WHOLE LOTTA CORNA'S GONNA BE UP FO' GRABS.
LISTEN TO YO ASS, LIKE YOU BE FITTIN' TO MAKE A PLAY IN THE DOPE GAME, SHIT.
OH. HEY, MAMA.
ANY YOU BOYS SEE WHO DONE THIS?
I DID.
BDEEP BDEEP
YO.

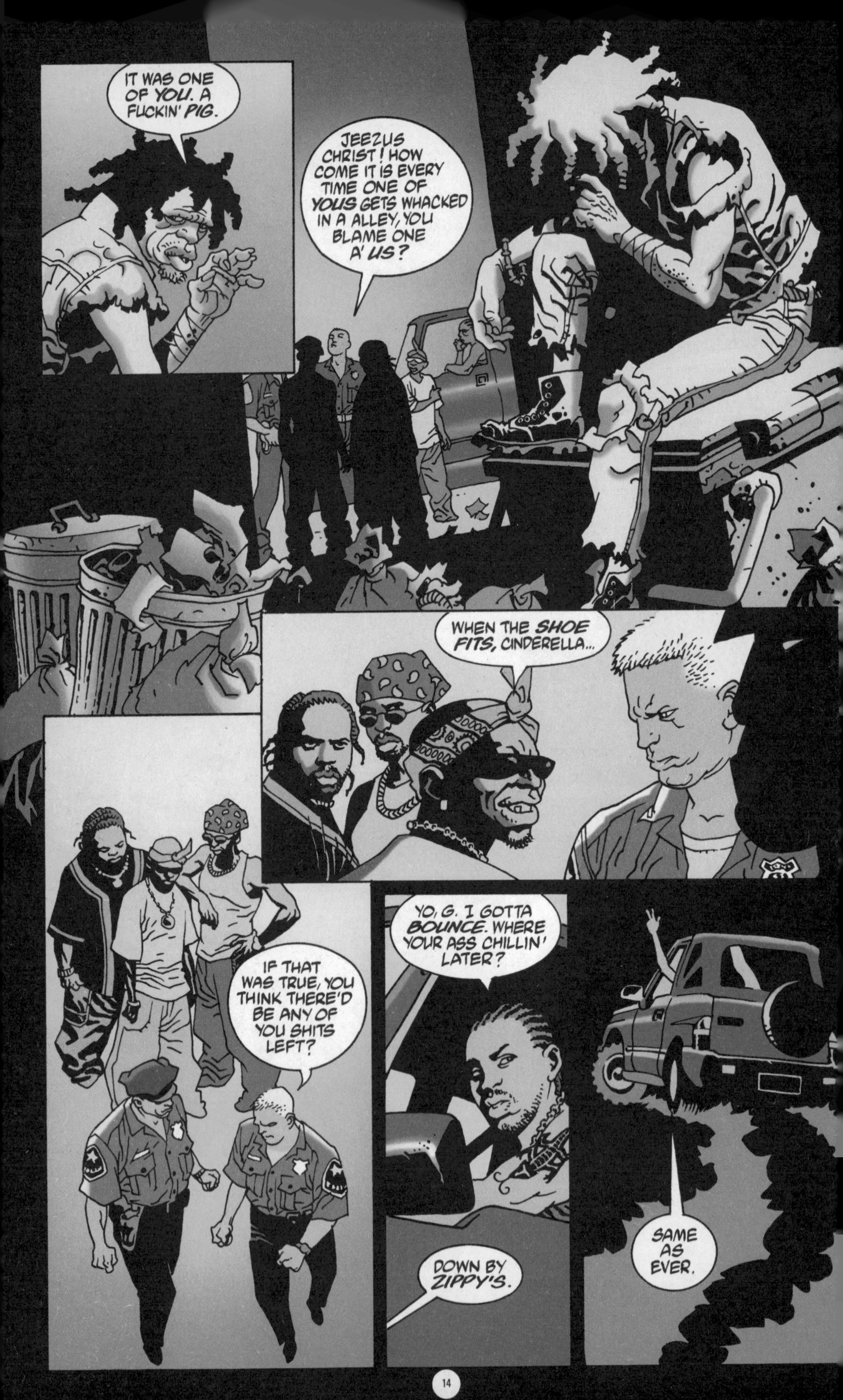

IT WAS ONE OF YOU. A FUCKIN' PIG.
JEEZUS CHRIST! HOW COME IT IS EVERY TIME ONE OF YOUS GETS WHACKED IN A ALLEY, YOU BLAME ONE A' US?
WHEN THE SHOE FITS, CINDERELLA...
IF THAT WAS TRUE, YOU THINK THERE'D BE ANY OF YOU SHITS LEFT?
YO, G. I GOTTA BOUNCE. WHERE YOUR ASS CHILLIN' LATER?
DOWN BY ZIPPY'S.
SAME AS EVER.

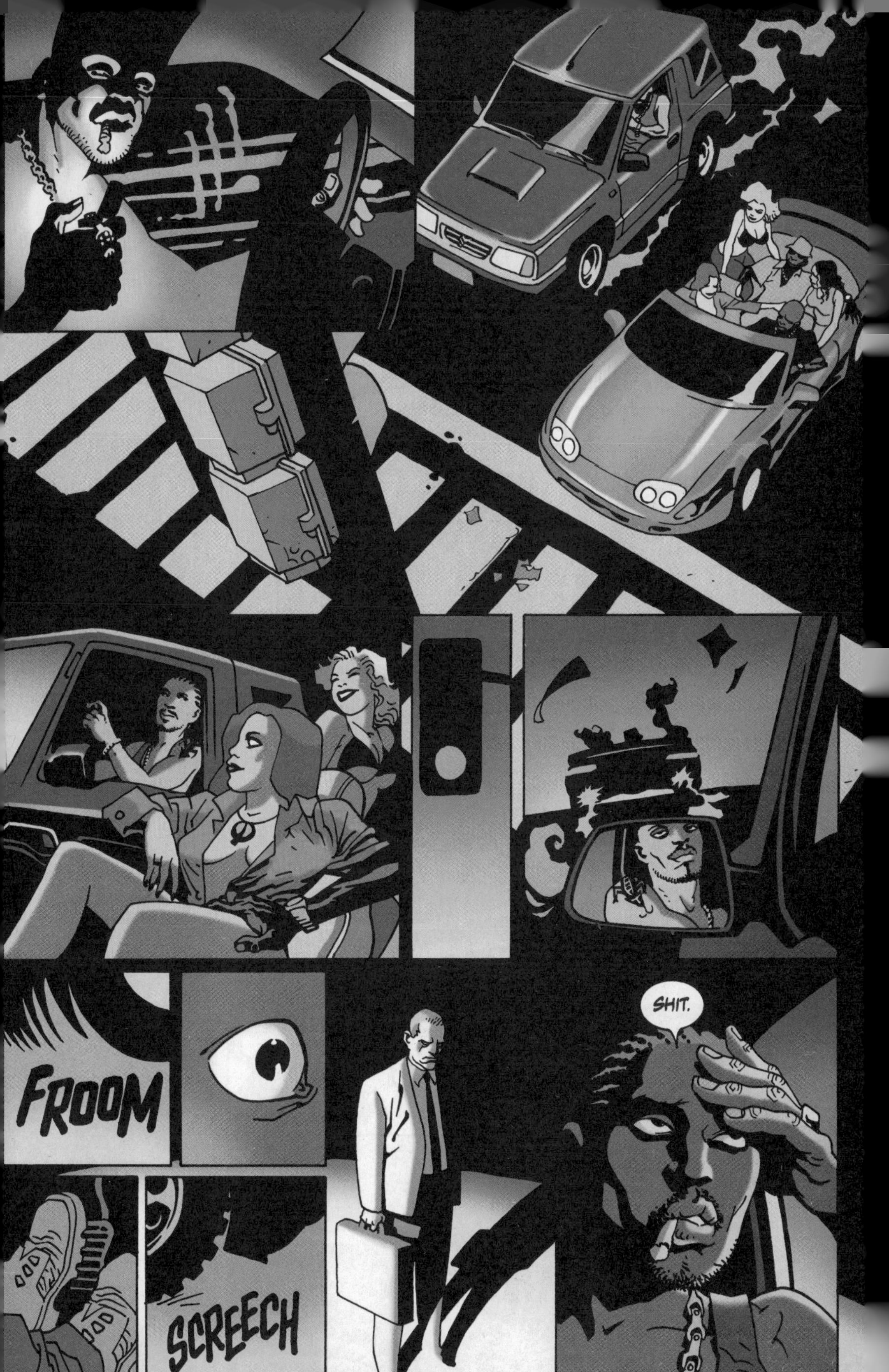
FROOM
SCREECH
SHIT.

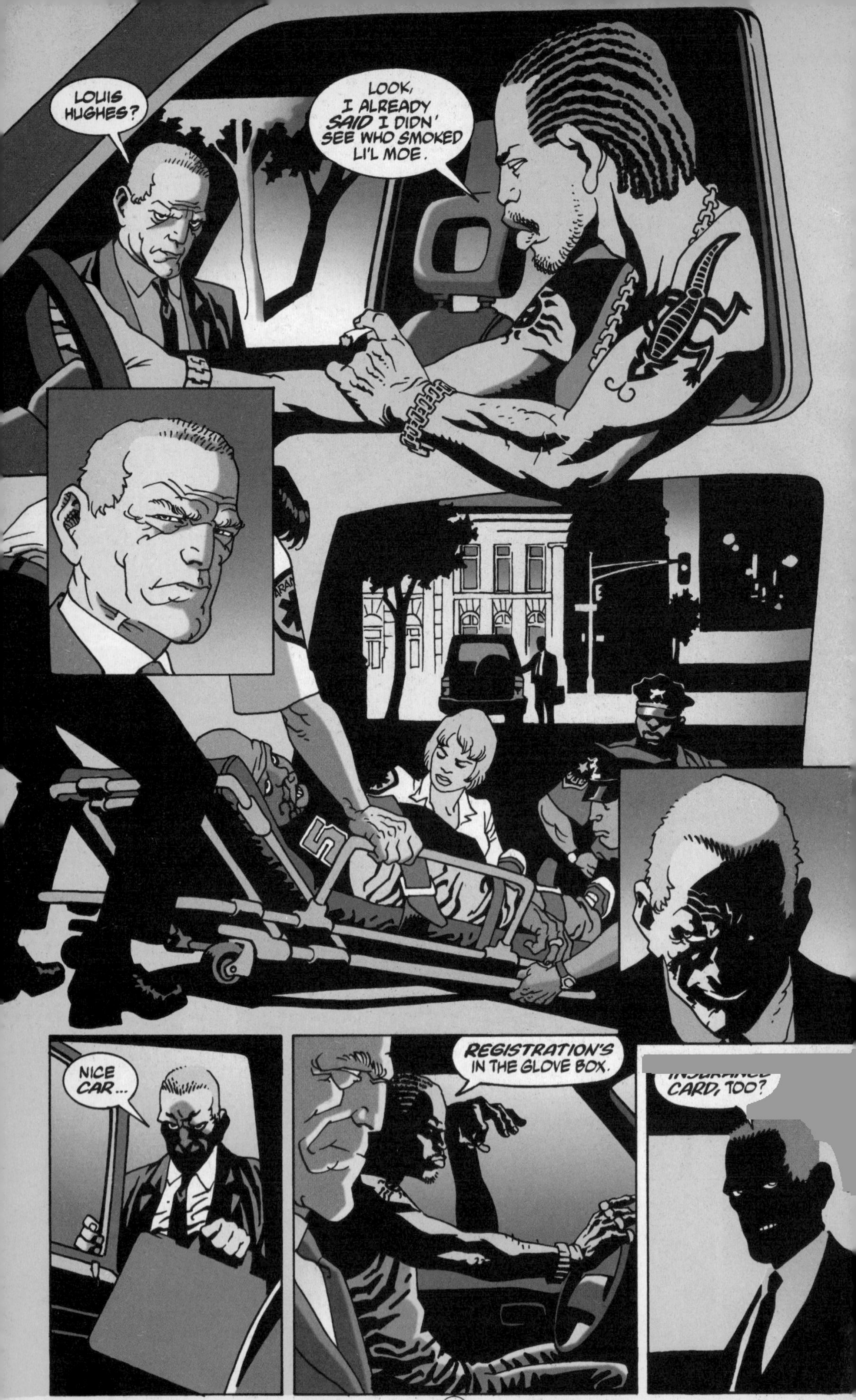
LOUIS HUGHES?
LOOK, I ALREADY SAID I DIDN' SEE WHO SMOKED LI'L MOE.
NICE CAR...
REGISTRATION'S IN THE GLOVE BOX.
CARD, TOO?

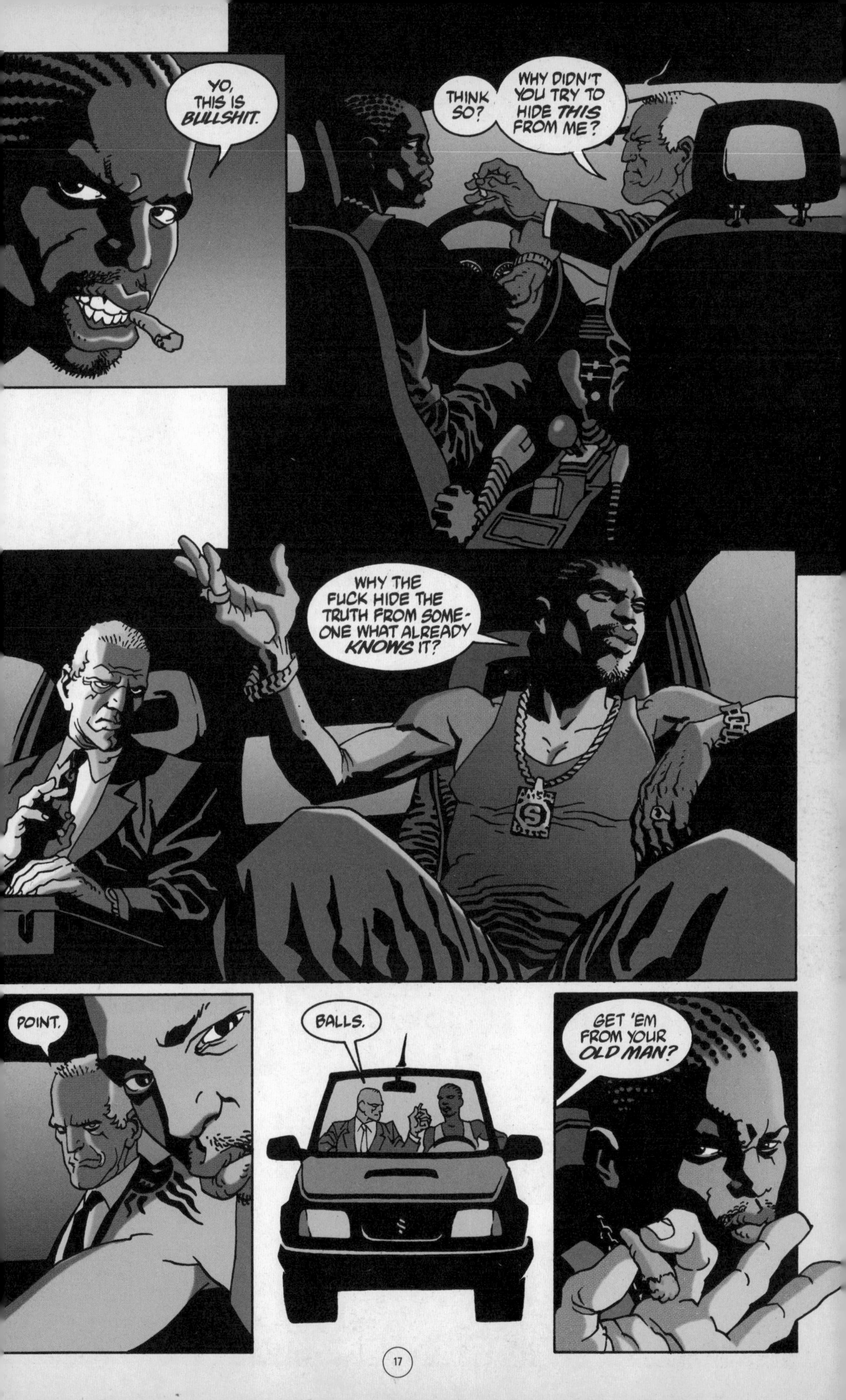
YO, THIS IS *BULLSHIT.*
THINK SO?
WHY DIDN'T YOU TRY TO HIDE *THIS* FROM ME?
WHY THE FUCK HIDE THE TRUTH FROM SOME-ONE WHAT ALREADY *KNOWS* IT?
POINT.
BALLS.
GET 'EM FROM YOUR *OLD MAN?*

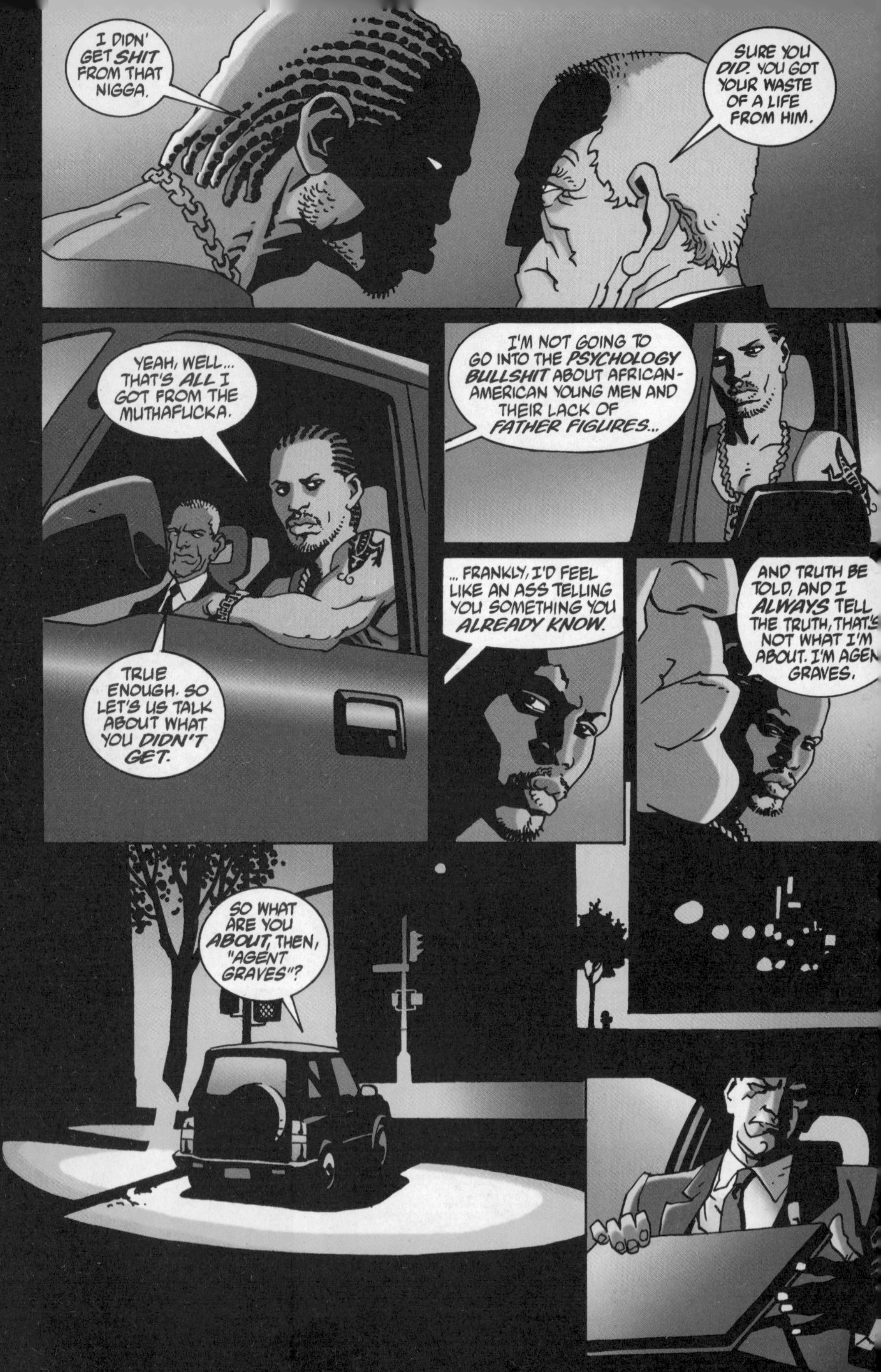
I DIDN' GET SHIT FROM THAT NIGGA.
SURE YOU DID. YOU GOT YOUR WASTE OF A LIFE FROM HIM.
YEAH, WELL... THAT'S ALL I GOT FROM THE MUTHAFUCKA.
TRUE ENOUGH. SO LET'S US TALK ABOUT WHAT YOU DIDN'T GET.
I'M NOT GOING TO GO INTO THE PSYCHOLOGY BULLSHIT ABOUT AFRICAN-AMERICAN YOUNG MEN AND THEIR LACK OF FATHER FIGURES...
... FRANKLY, I'D FEEL LIKE AN ASS TELLING YOU SOMETHING YOU ALREADY KNOW.
AND TRUTH BE TOLD, AND I ALWAYS TELL THE TRUTH, THAT'S NOT WHAT I'M ABOUT. I'M AGEN GRAVES.
SO WHAT ARE YOU ABOUT, THEN, "AGENT GRAVES"?

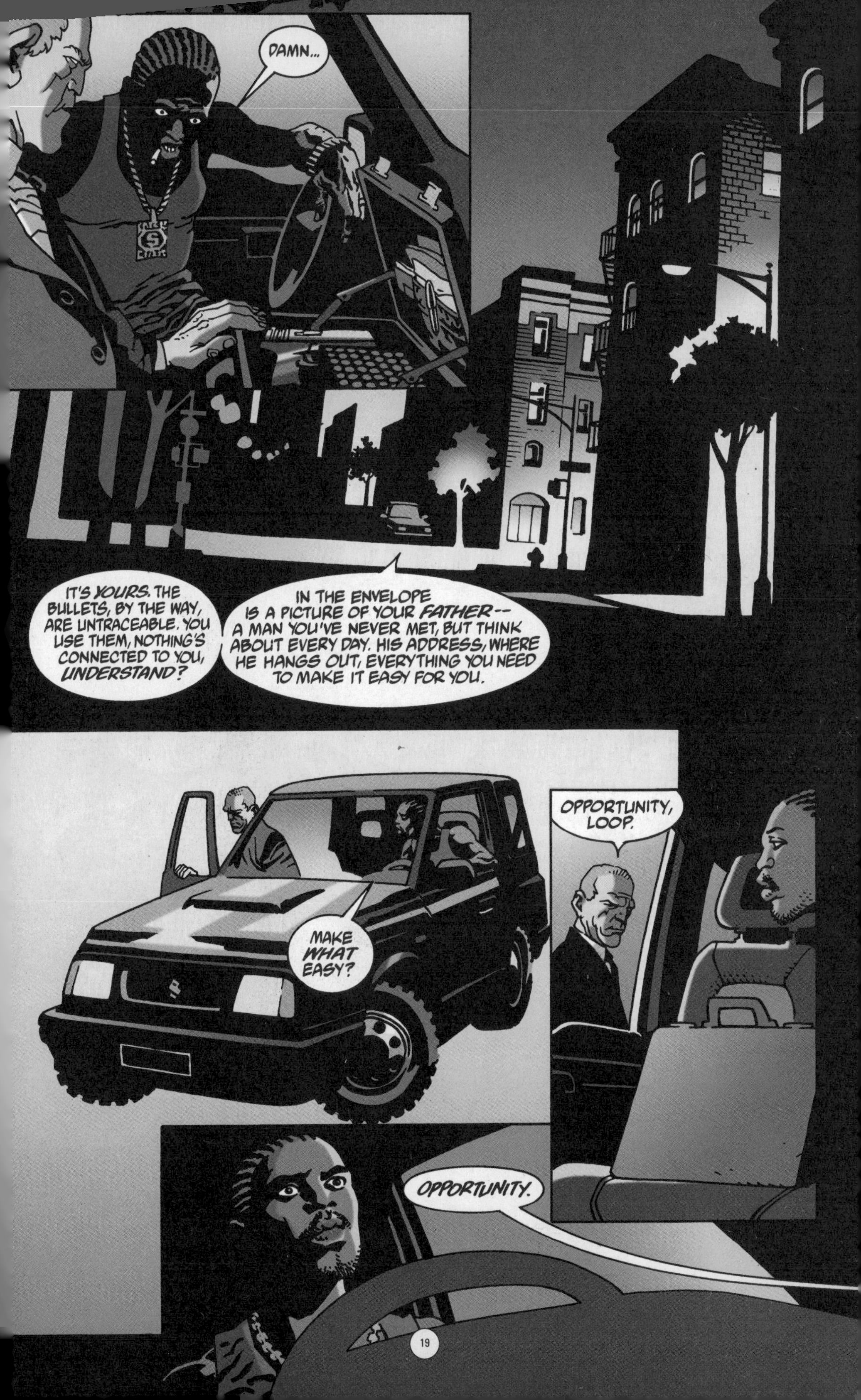
DAMN...
IT'S YOURS. THE BULLETS, BY THE WAY, ARE UNTRACEABLE. YOU USE THEM, NOTHING'S CONNECTED TO YOU, UNDERSTAND?
IN THE ENVELOPE IS A PICTURE OF YOUR FATHER-- A MAN YOU'VE NEVER MET, BUT THINK ABOUT EVERY DAY. HIS ADDRESS, WHERE HE HANGS OUT, EVERYTHING YOU NEED TO MAKE IT EASY FOR YOU.
MAKE WHAT EASY?
OPPORTUNITY, LOOP.
OPPORTUNITY.

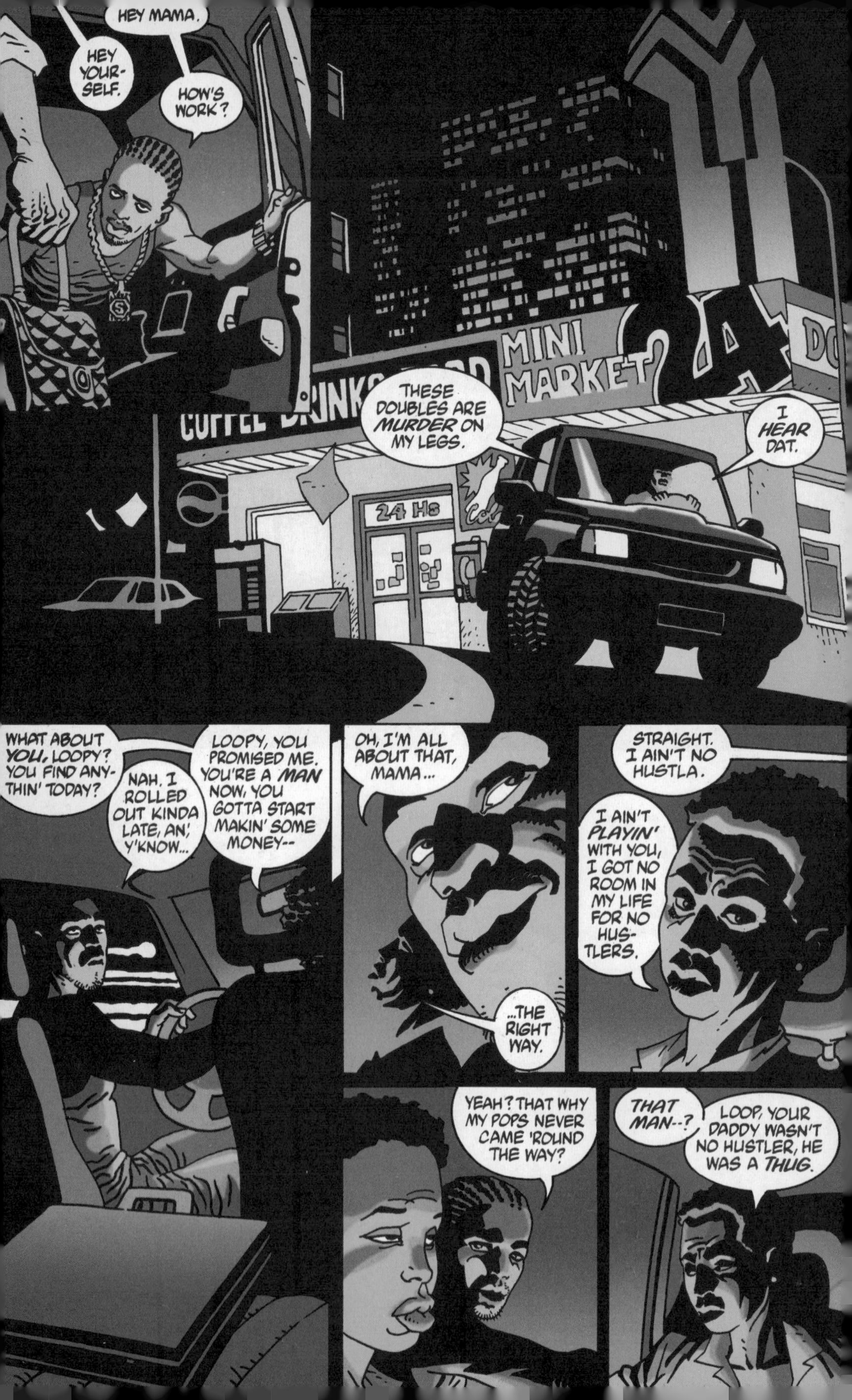
HEY MAMA.
HEY YOURSELF.
HOW'S WORK?
MINI MARKET
COFFEE DRINKS
24 Hs
THESE DOUBLES ARE MURDER ON MY LEGS.
I HEAR DAT.
WHAT ABOUT YOU, LOOPY? YOU FIND ANYTHIN' TODAY?
NAH. I ROLLED OUT KINDA LATE, AN', Y'KNOW...
LOOPY, YOU PROMISED ME. YOU'RE A MAN NOW, YOU GOTTA START MAKIN' SOME MONEY--
OH, I'M ALL ABOUT THAT, MAMA...
...THE RIGHT WAY.
STRAIGHT. I AIN'T NO HUSTLA.
I AIN'T PLAYIN' WITH YOU, I GOT NO ROOM IN MY LIFE FOR NO HUSTLERS.
YEAH? THAT WHY MY POPS NEVER CAME 'ROUND THE WAY?
THAT MAN--?
LOOP, YOUR DADDY WASN'T NO HUSTLER, HE WAS A THUG.

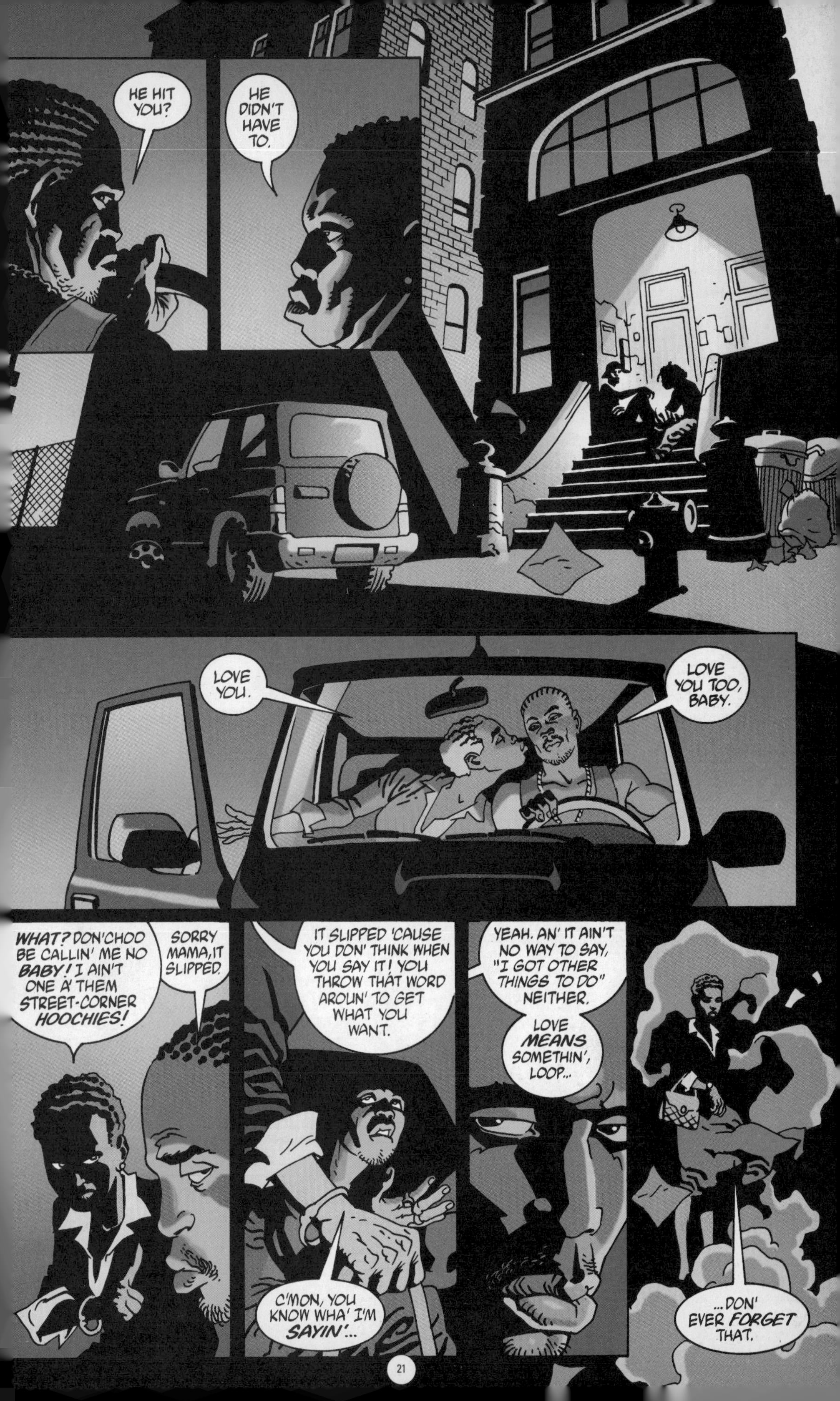
HE HIT YOU?
HE DIDN'T HAVE TO.
LOVE YOU.
LOVE YOU TOO, BABY.
WHAT? DON'CHOO BE CALLIN' ME NO BABY! I AIN'T ONE A' THEM STREET-CORNER HOOCHIES!
SORRY MAMA, IT SLIPPED.
IT SLIPPED 'CAUSE YOU DON' THINK WHEN YOU SAY IT! YOU THROW THAT WORD AROUN' TO GET WHAT YOU WANT.
C'MON, YOU KNOW WHA' I'M SAYIN'...
YEAH. AN' IT AIN'T NO WAY TO SAY, "I GOT OTHER THINGS TO DO" NEITHER.
LOVE MEANS SOMETHIN', LOOP...
...DON' EVER FORGET THAT.

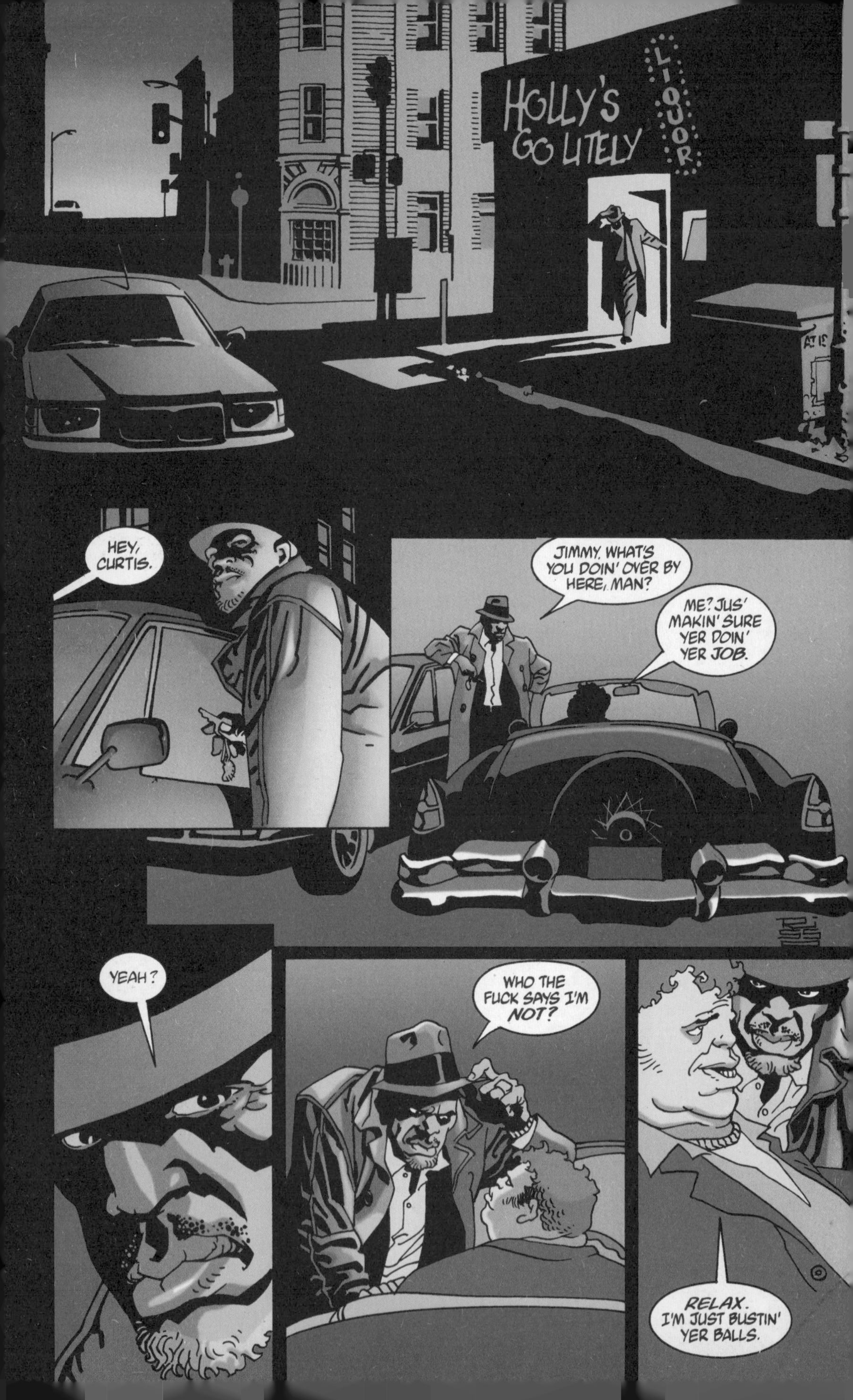
HOLLY'S GO LITELY
LIQUOR
HEY, CURTIS.
JIMMY. WHAT'S YOU DOIN' OVER BY HERE, MAN?
ME? JUS' MAKIN' SURE YER DOIN' YER JOB.
YEAH?
WHO THE FUCK SAYS I'M NOT?
RELAX. I'M JUST BUSTIN' YER BALLS.

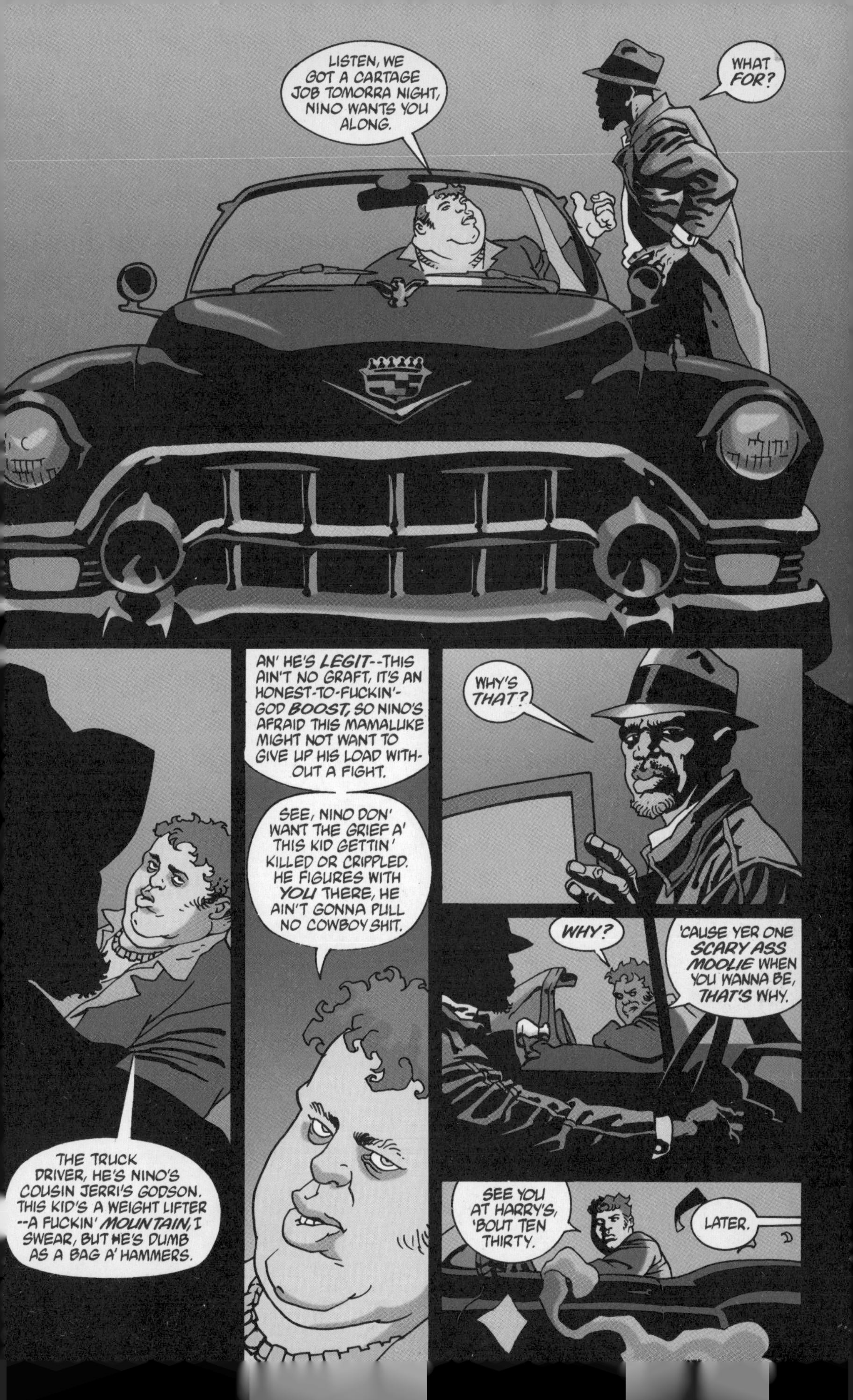

LISTEN, WE GOT A CARTAGE JOB TOMORRA NIGHT, NINO WANTS YOU ALONG.
WHAT FOR?
THE TRUCK DRIVER, HE'S NINO'S COUSIN JERRI'S GODSON. THIS KID'S A WEIGHT LIFTER --A FUCKIN' MOUNTAIN, I SWEAR, BUT HE'S DUMB AS A BAG A' HAMMERS.
AN' HE'S LEGIT--THIS AIN'T NO GRAFT, IT'S AN HONEST-TO-FUCKIN'-GOD BOOST, SO NINO'S AFRAID THIS MAMALUKE MIGHT NOT WANT TO GIVE UP HIS LOAD WITH-OUT A FIGHT.
SEE, NINO DON' WANT THE GRIEF A' THIS KID GETTIN' KILLED OR CRIPPLED. HE FIGURES WITH YOU THERE, HE AIN'T GONNA PULL NO COWBOY SHIT.
WHY'S THAT?
WHY?
'CAUSE YER ONE SCARY ASS MOOLIE WHEN YOU WANNA BE, THAT'S WHY.
SEE YOU AT HARRY'S, 'BOUT TEN THIRTY.
LATER.

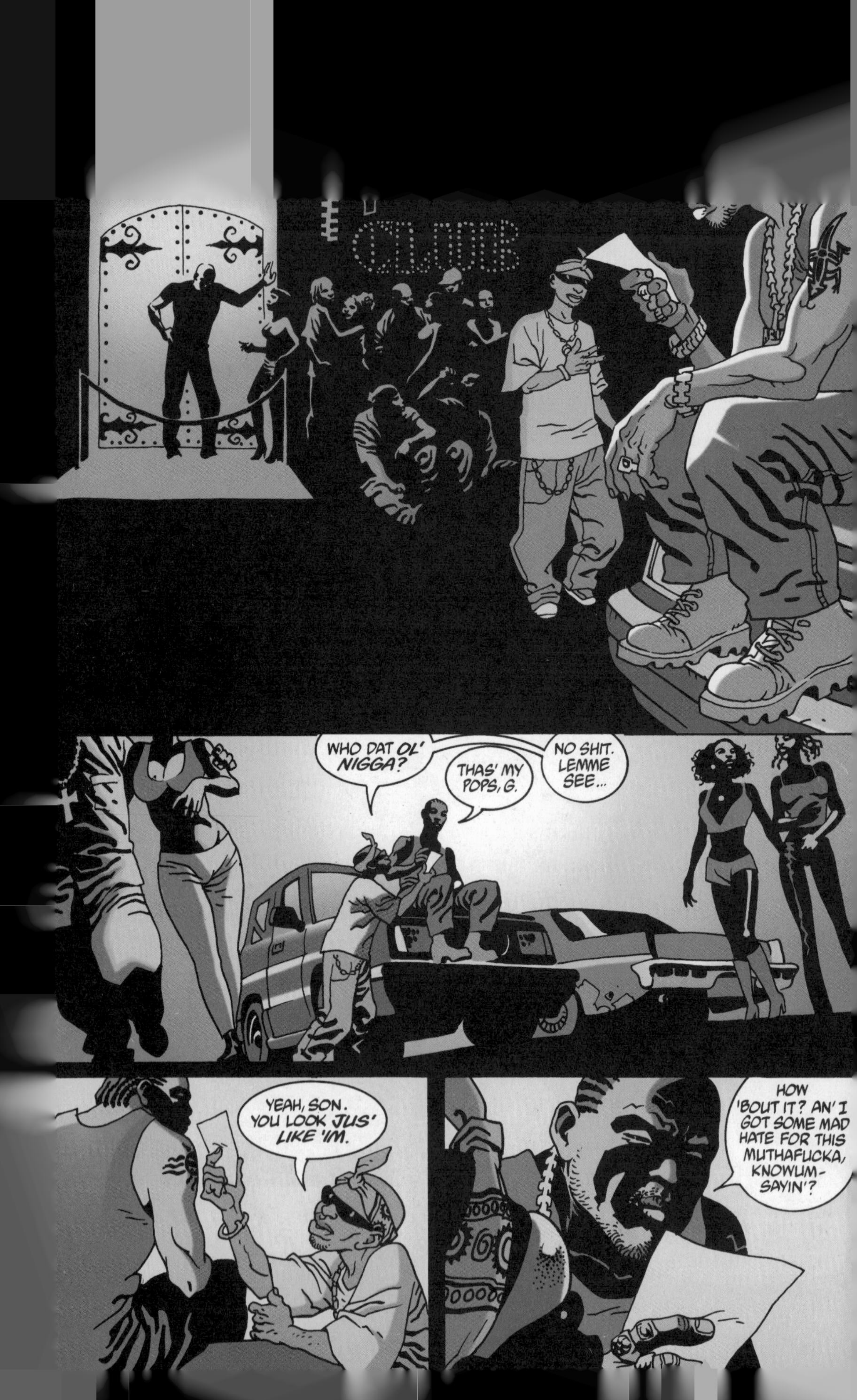
WHO DAT OL' NIGGA?
THAS' MY POPS, G.
NO SHIT. LEMME SEE...
YEAH, SON. YOU LOOK JUS' LIKE 'IM.
HOW 'BOUT IT? AN' I GOT SOME MAD HATE FOR THIS MUTHAFUCKA, KNOWUM-SAYIN'?

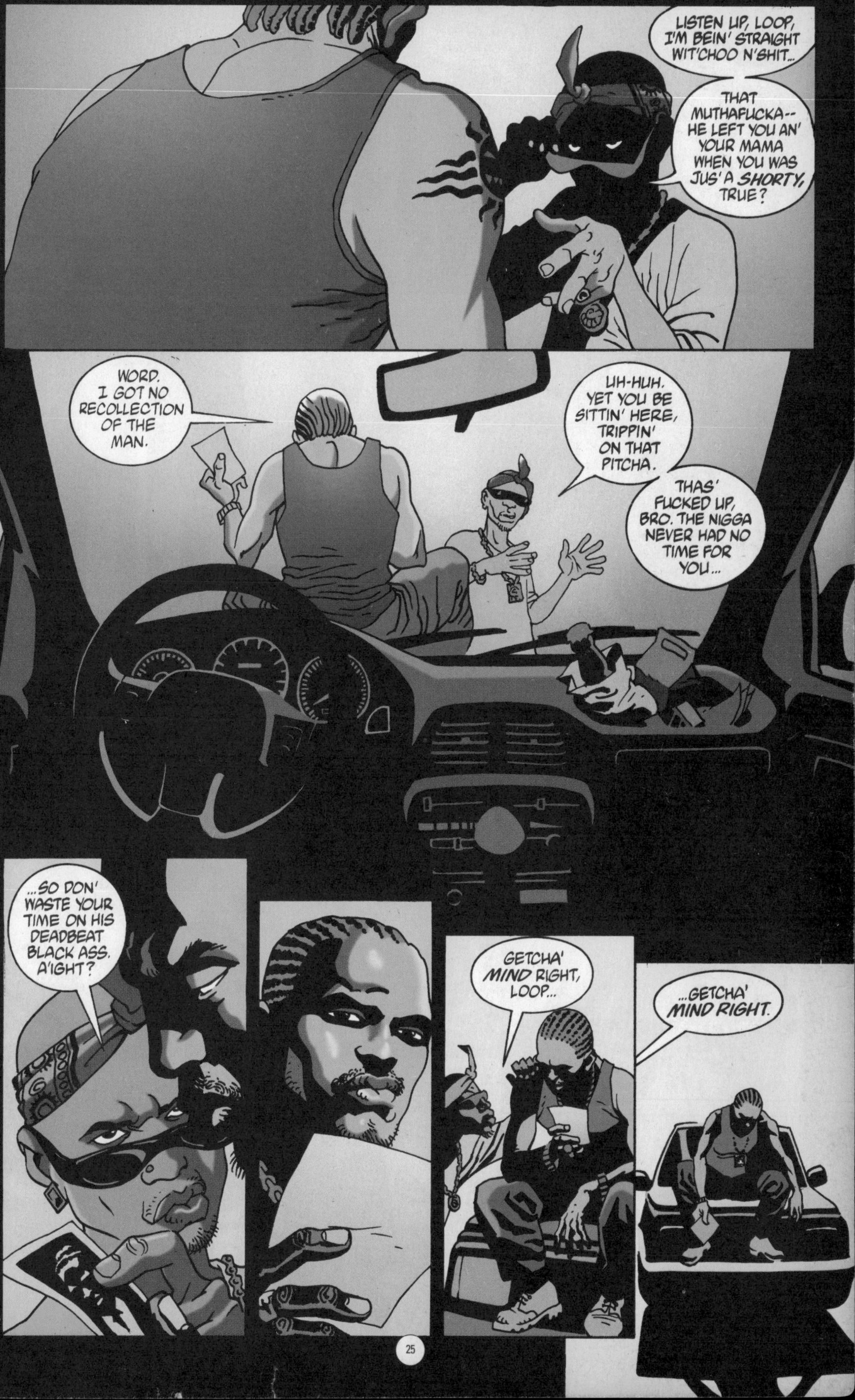
LISTEN UP, LOOP, I'M BEIN' STRAIGHT WIT'CHOO N'SHIT...
THAT MUTHAFUCKA-- HE LEFT YOU AN' YOUR MAMA WHEN YOU WAS JUS' A SHORTY, TRUE?
WORD. I GOT NO RECOLLECTION OF THE MAN.
UH-HUH. YET YOU BE SITTIN' HERE, TRIPPIN' ON THAT PITCHA.
THAS' FUCKED UP, BRO. THE NIGGA NEVER HAD NO TIME FOR YOU...
...SO DON' WASTE YOUR TIME ON HIS DEADBEAT BLACK ASS. A'IGHT?
GETCHA' MIND RIGHT, LOOP...
...GETCHA' MIND RIGHT.

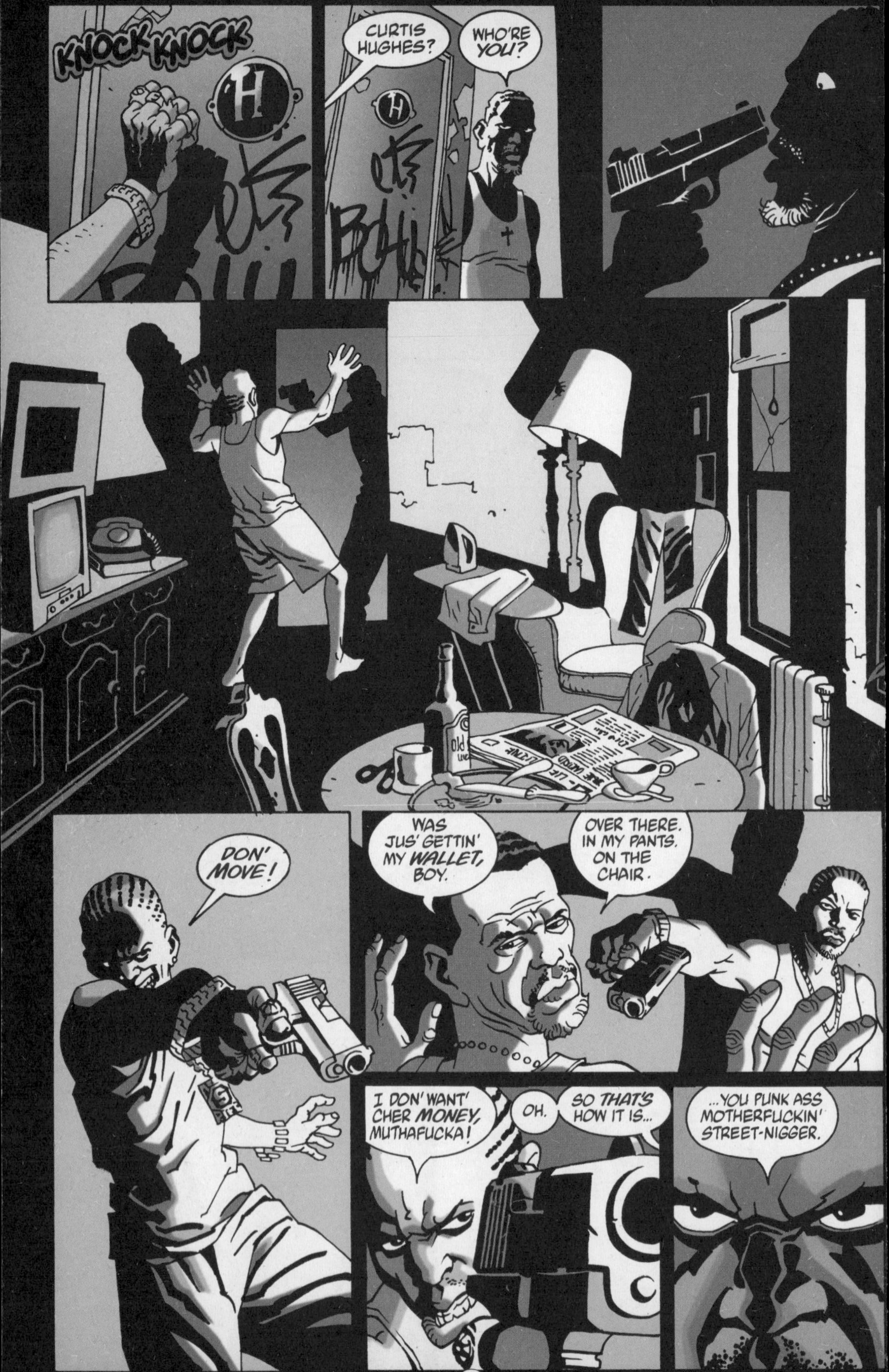
KNOCK KNOCK
CURTIS HUGHES?
WHO'RE YOU?
DON' MOVE!
WAS JUS' GETTIN' MY WALLET, BOY.
OVER THERE. IN MY PANTS. ON THE CHAIR.
I DON' WANT' CHER MONEY, MUTHAFUCKA!
OH.
SO THAT'S HOW IT IS...
...YOU PUNK ASS MOTHERFUCKIN' STREET-NIGGER.

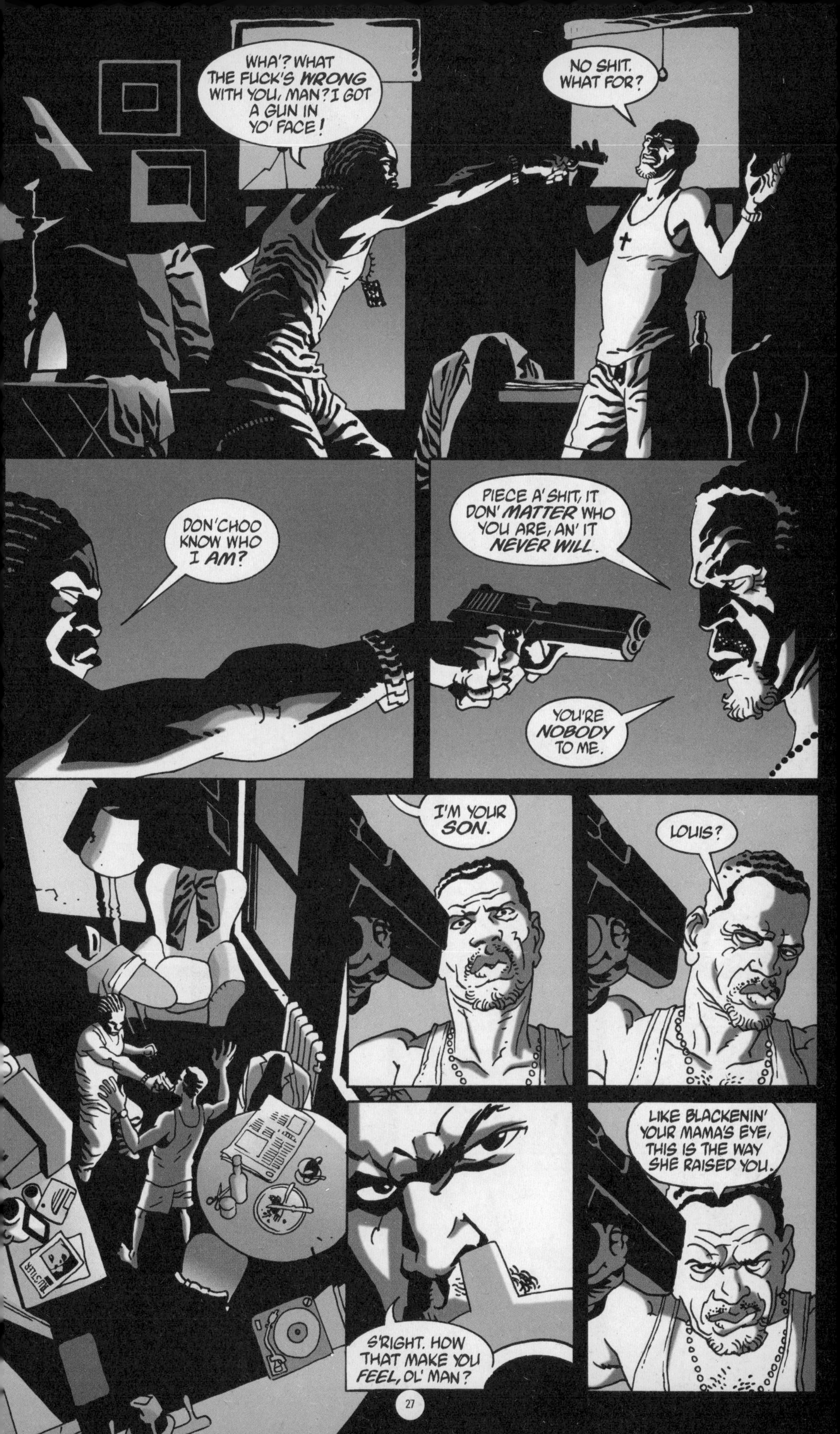
WHA'? WHAT THE FUCK'S **WRONG** WITH YOU, MAN? I GOT A GUN IN YO' FACE!
NO SHIT. WHAT FOR?
DON'CHOO KNOW WHO I **AM**?
PIECE A' SHIT, IT DON' **MATTER** WHO YOU ARE, AN' IT **NEVER WILL**.
YOU'RE **NOBODY** TO ME.
I'M YOUR **SON**.
LOUIS?
S'RIGHT. HOW THAT MAKE YOU **FEEL**, OL' MAN?
LIKE BLACKENIN' YOUR MAMA'S EYE, THIS IS THE WAY SHE RAISED YOU.
HUSTLER

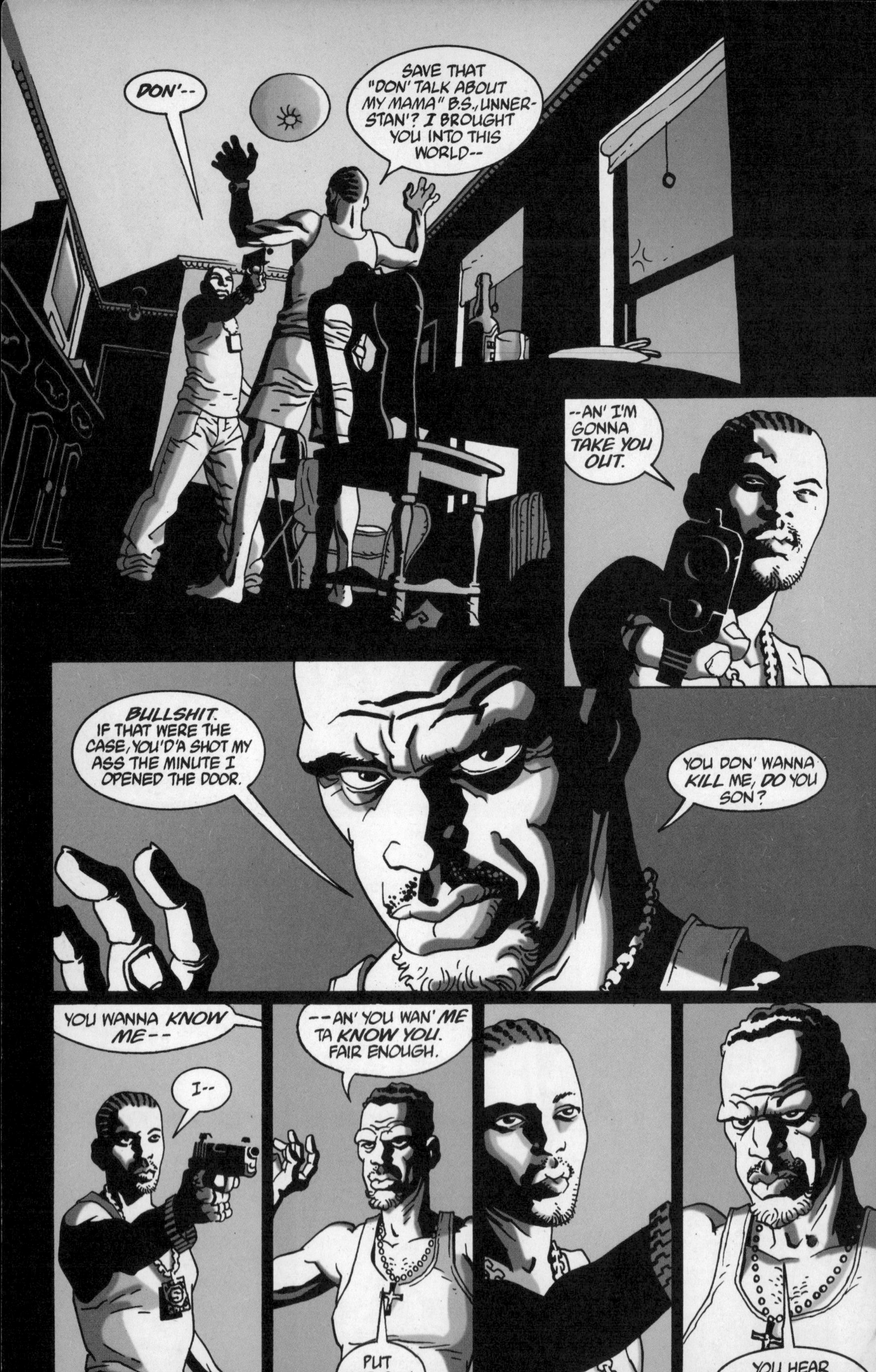
DON'--
SAVE THAT "DON' TALK ABOUT MY MAMA" B.S., UNNER-STAN'? I BROUGHT YOU INTO THIS WORLD--
--AN' I'M GONNA TAKE YOU OUT.
BULLSHIT. IF THAT WERE THE CASE, YOU'D'A SHOT MY ASS THE MINUTE I OPENED THE DOOR.
YOU DON' WANNA KILL ME, DO YOU SON?
YOU WANNA KNOW ME--
I--
--AN' YOU WAN' ME TA KNOW YOU. FAIR ENOUGH.
PUT THE GUN DOWN.
YOU HEAR ME? I SAID PUT THE GUN DOWN.

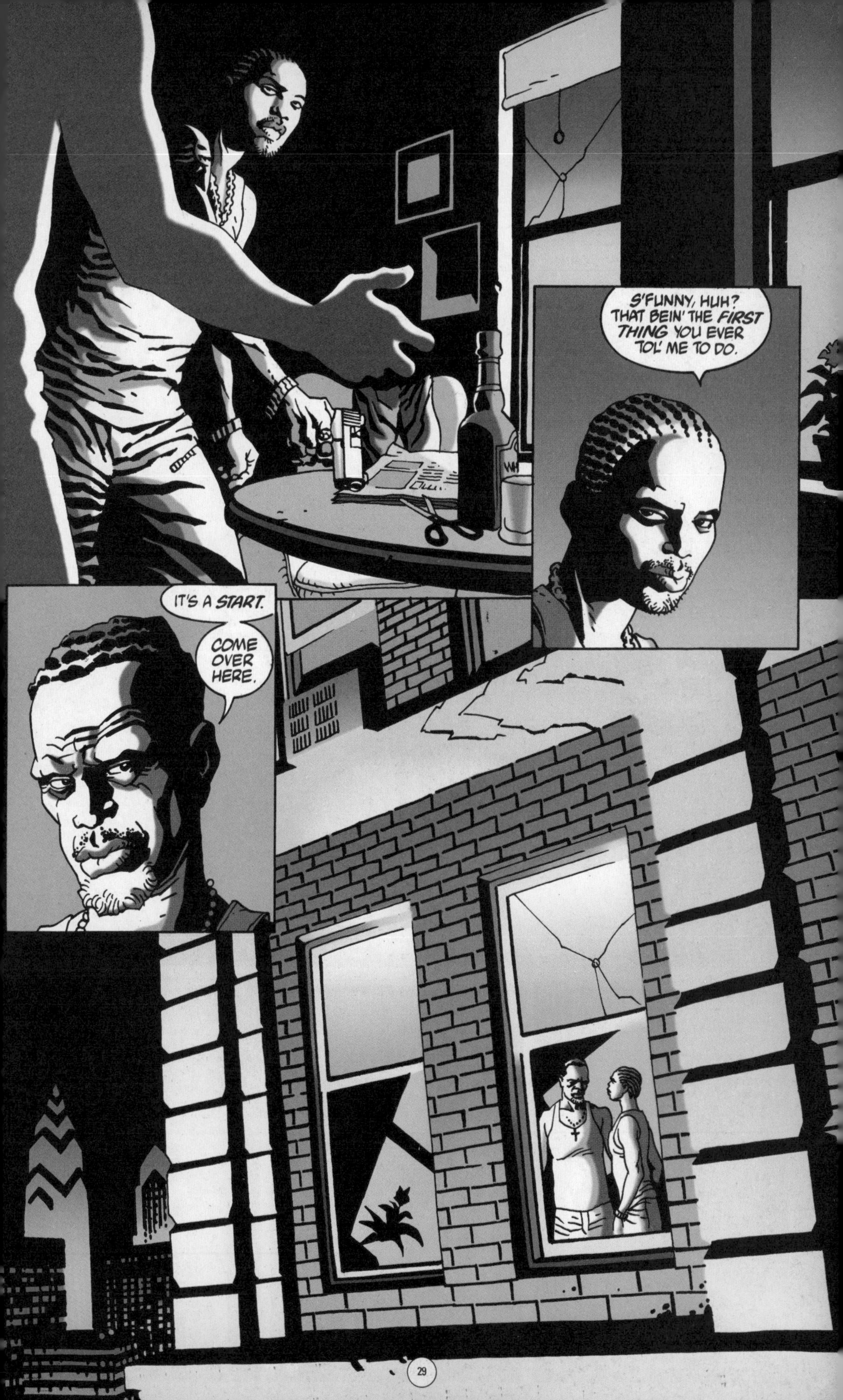
S'FUNNY, HUH? THAT BEIN' THE FIRST THING YOU EVER TOL' ME TO DO.
IT'S A START.
COME OVER HERE.

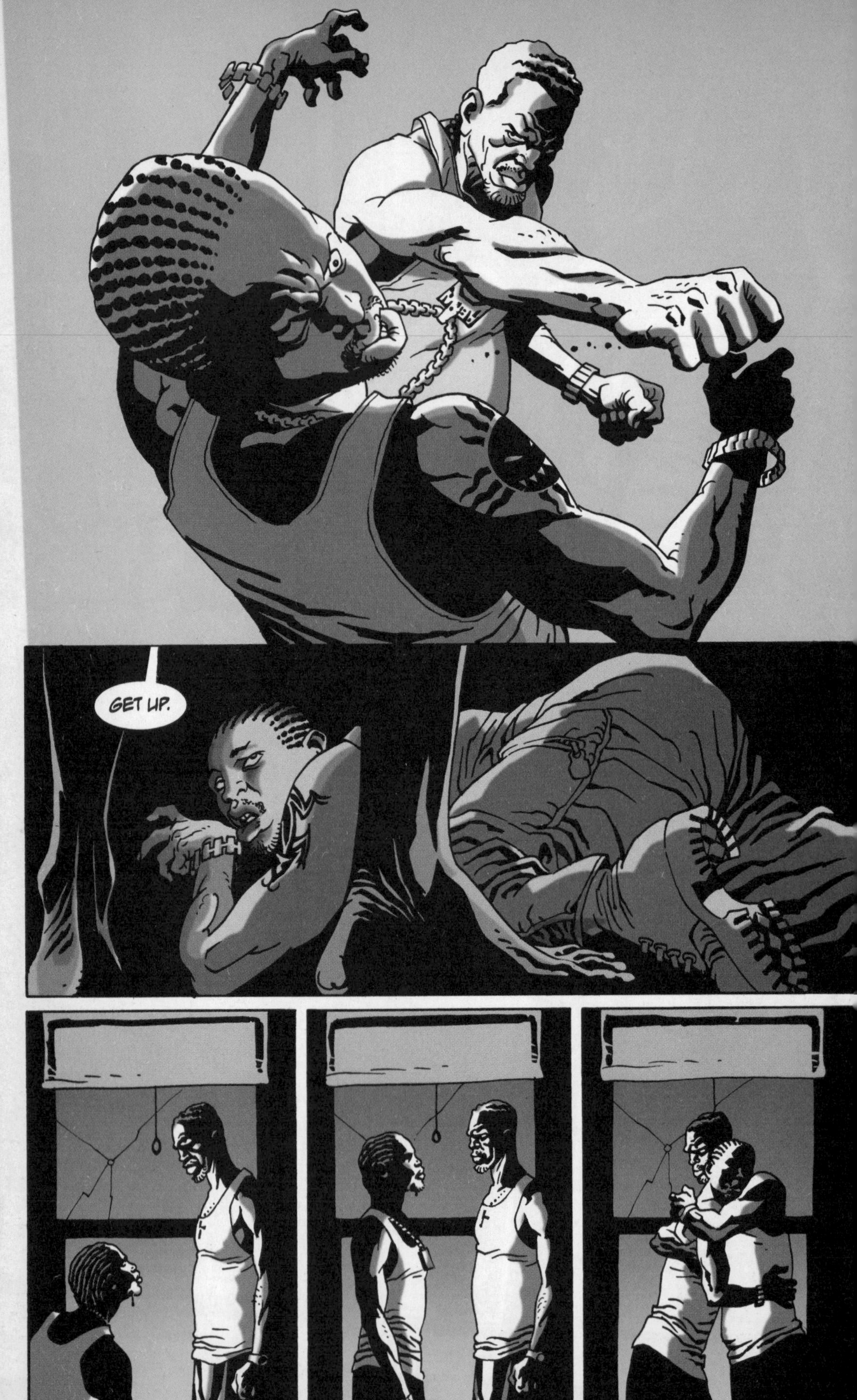
GET UP.

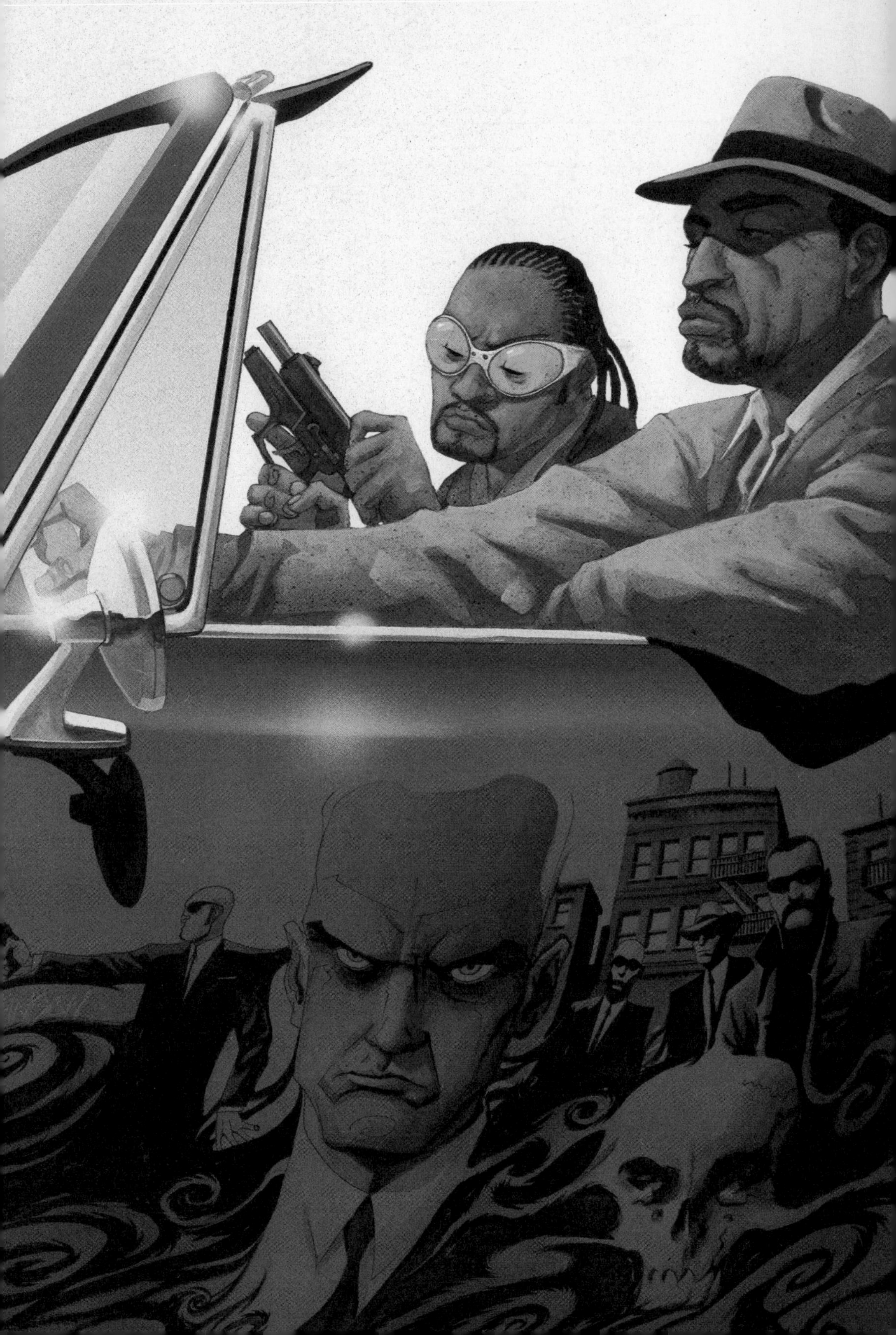

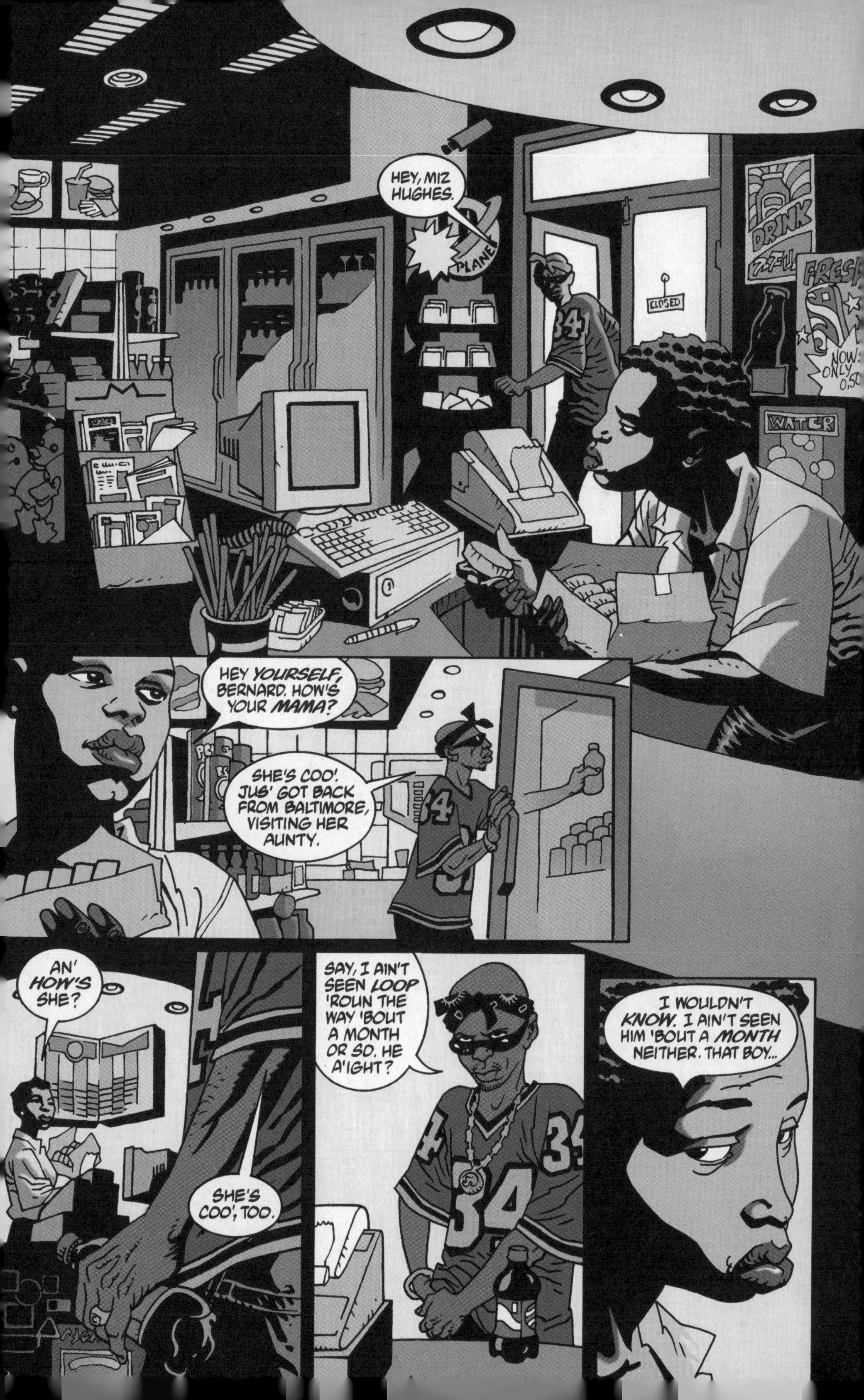
HEY, MIZ HUGHES.
PLANET
CLOSED
DRINK
FRESH
NOW! ONLY 0.50
WATER
HEY YOURSELF, BERNARD. HOW'S YOUR MAMA?
SHE'S COO'. JUS' GOT BACK FROM BALTIMORE, VISITING HER AUNTY.
AN' HOW'S SHE?
SHE'S COO', TOO.
SAY, I AIN'T SEEN LOOP 'ROUN THE WAY 'BOUT A MONTH OR SO. HE A'IGHT?
I WOULDN'T KNOW. I AIN'T SEEN HIM 'BOUT A MONTH NEITHER. THAT BOY...

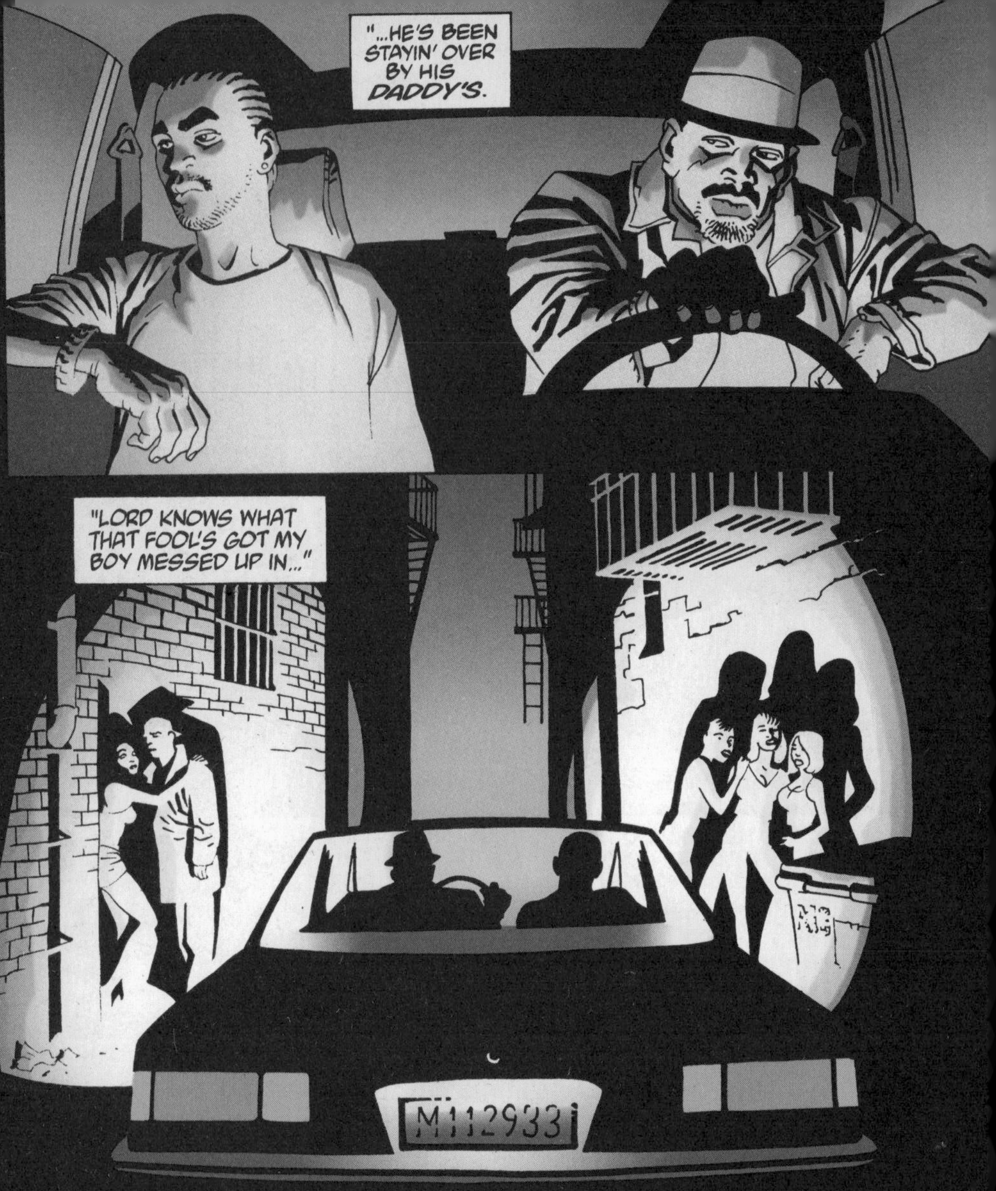
"...HE'S BEEN STAYIN' OVER BY HIS DADDY'S.
"LORD KNOWS WHAT THAT FOOL'S GOT MY BOY MESSED UP IN..."
M112933

HANG UP ON THE HANG LOW PART TWO

BRIAN AZZARELLO, writer EDUARDO RISSO, artist

PATRICIA MULVIHILL, colorist DIGITAL CHAMELEON, separations CLEM ROBINS, letters
DAVE JOHNSON, cover JENNIFER LEE, ass't editor AXEL ALONSO, editor

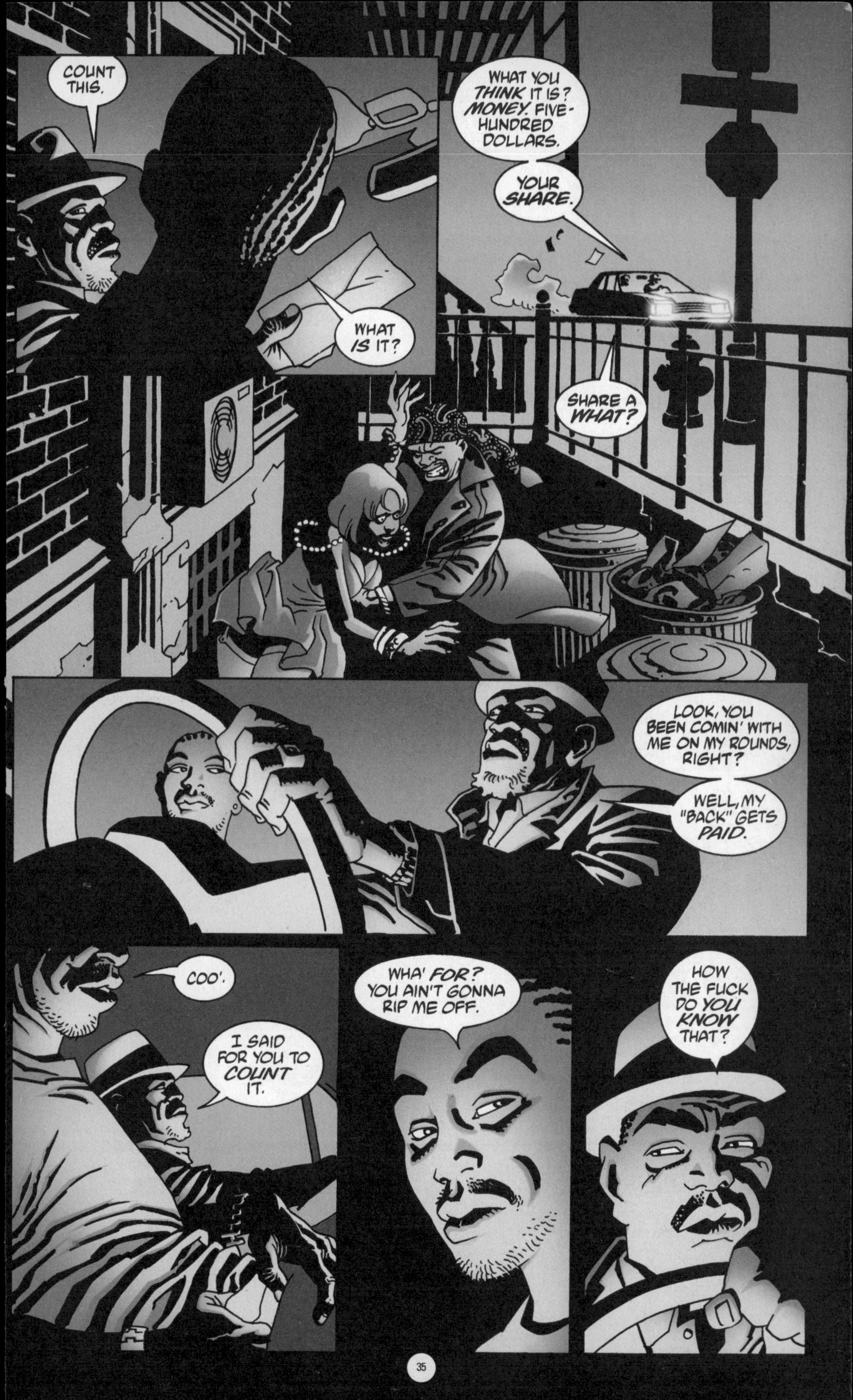
COUNT THIS.
WHAT IS IT?
WHAT YOU THINK IT IS? MONEY. FIVE-HUNDRED DOLLARS.
YOUR SHARE.
SHARE A WHAT?
LOOK, YOU BEEN COMIN' WITH ME ON MY ROUNDS, RIGHT?
WELL, MY "BACK" GETS PAID.
COO'.
I SAID FOR YOU TO COUNT IT.
WHA' FOR? YOU AIN'T GONNA RIP ME OFF.
HOW THE FUCK DO YOU KNOW THAT?

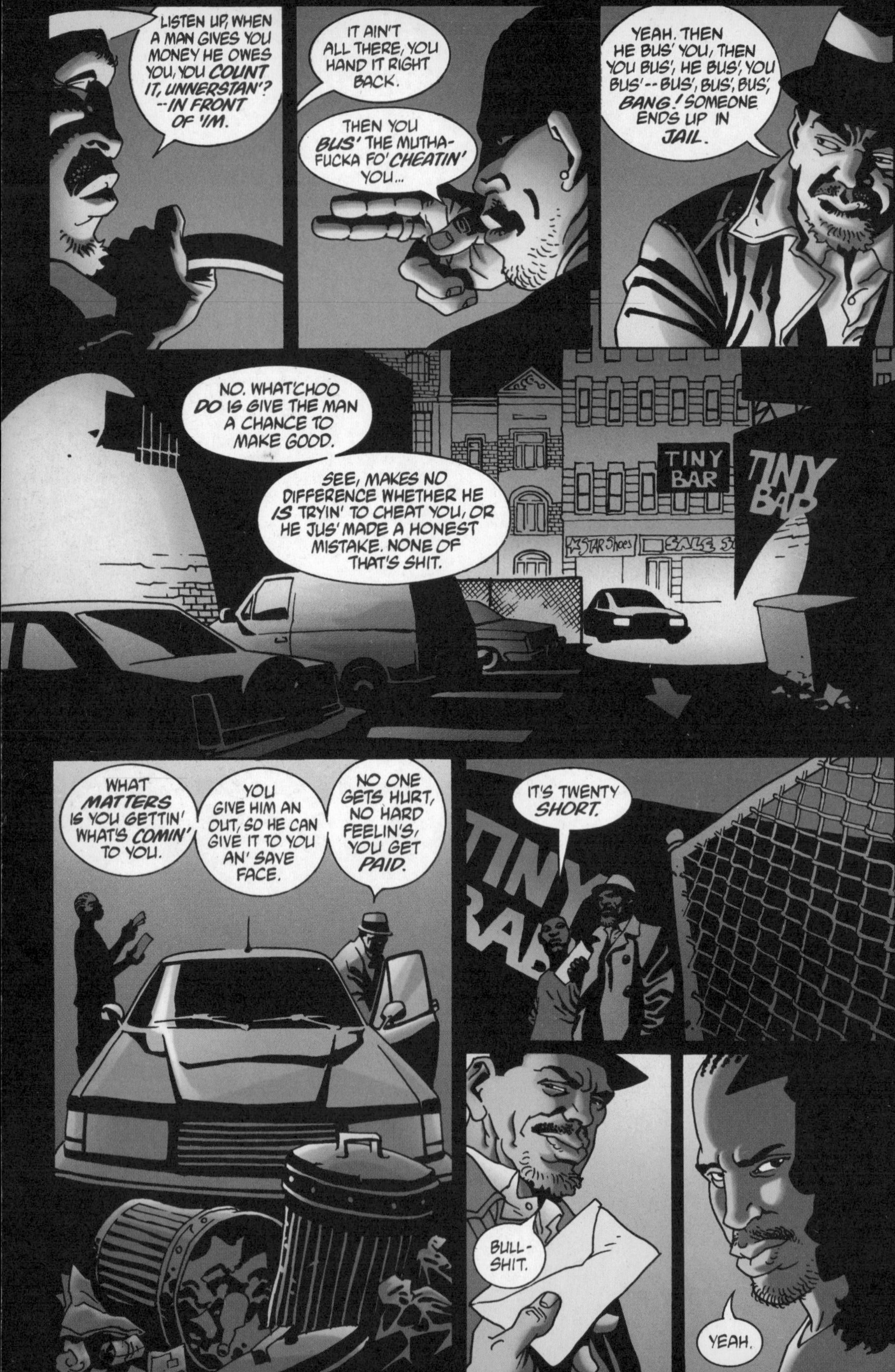

LISTEN UP, WHEN A MAN GIVES YOU MONEY HE OWES YOU, YOU COUNT IT, UNNERSTAN'? --IN FRONT OF 'IM.
IT AIN'T ALL THERE, YOU HAND IT RIGHT BACK.
THEN YOU BUS' THE MUTHA-FUCKA FO' CHEATIN' YOU...
YEAH. THEN HE BUS' YOU, THEN YOU BUS', HE BUS', YOU BUS'-- BUS', BUS', BUS', BANG! SOMEONE ENDS UP IN JAIL.
NO. WHAT'CHOO DO IS GIVE THE MAN A CHANCE TO MAKE GOOD.
SEE, MAKES NO DIFFERENCE WHETHER HE IS TRYIN' TO CHEAT YOU, OR HE JUS' MADE A HONEST MISTAKE. NONE OF THAT'S SHIT.
TINY BAR
TINY BAR
STAR Shoes
WHAT MATTERS IS YOU GETTIN' WHAT'S COMIN' TO YOU.
YOU GIVE HIM AN OUT, SO HE CAN GIVE IT TO YOU AN' SAVE FACE.
NO ONE GETS HURT, NO HARD FEELIN'S, YOU GET PAID.
IT'S TWENTY SHORT.
BULL-SHIT.
YEAH.

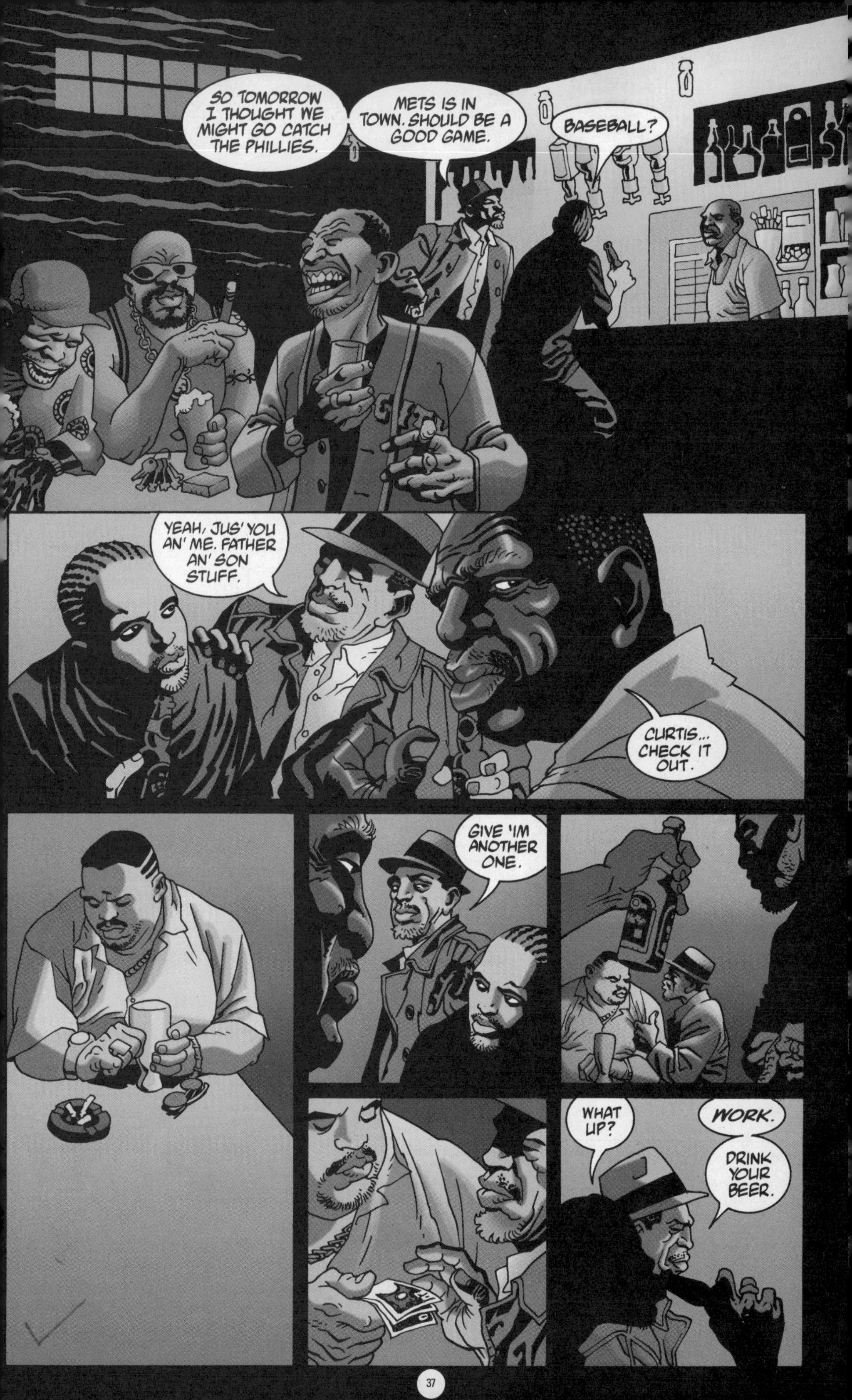

SO TOMORROW I THOUGHT WE MIGHT GO CATCH THE PHILLIES.
METS IS IN TOWN. SHOULD BE A GOOD GAME.
BASEBALL?
YEAH, JUS' YOU AN' ME. FATHER AN' SON STUFF.
CURTIS... CHECK IT OUT.
GIVE 'IM ANOTHER ONE.
WHAT UP?
WORK.
DRINK YOUR BEER.

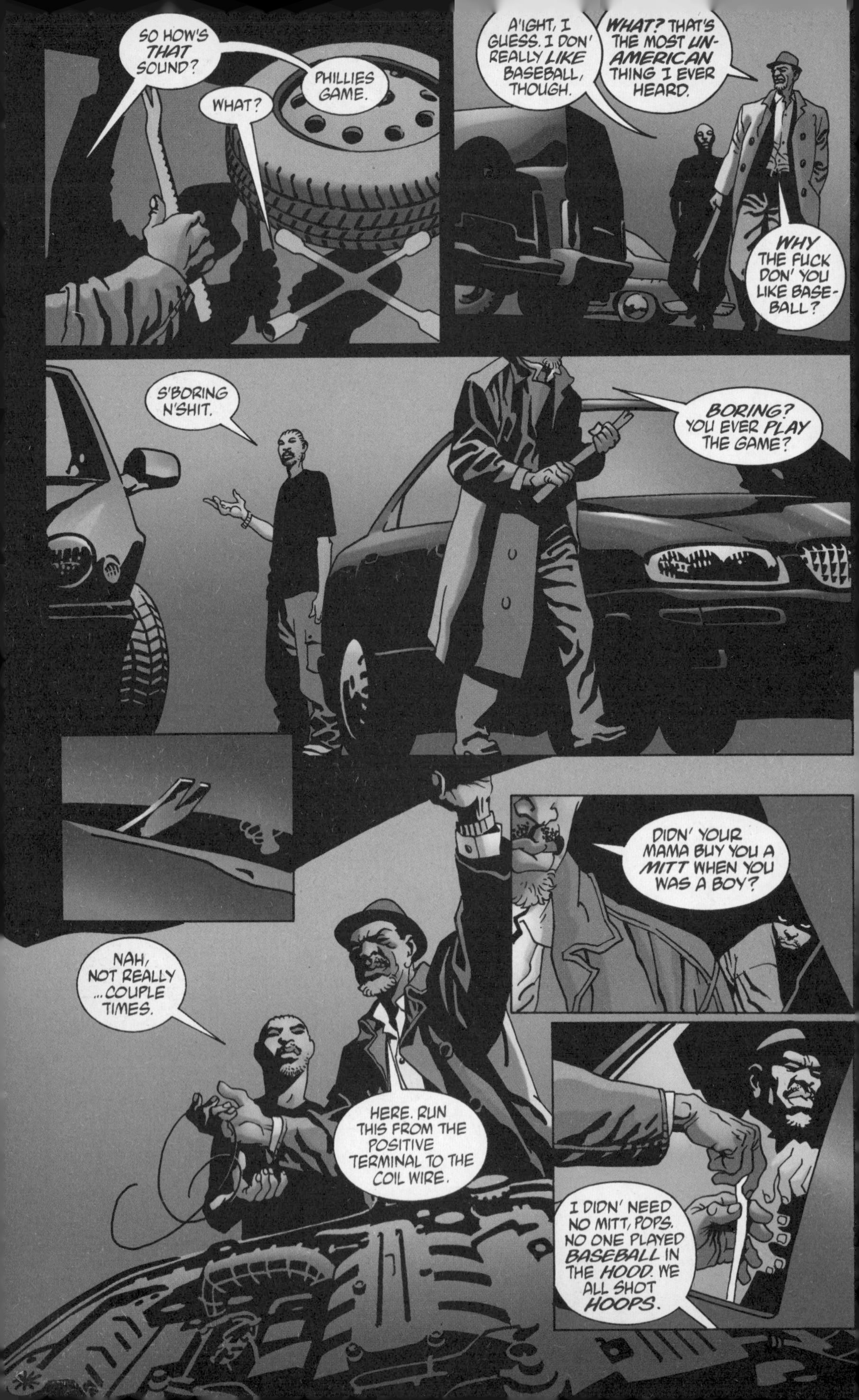
SO HOW'S THAT SOUND?
WHAT?
PHILLIES GAME.
A'IGHT, I GUESS. I DON' REALLY LIKE BASEBALL, THOUGH.
WHAT? THAT'S THE MOST UN-AMERICAN THING I EVER HEARD.
WHY THE FUCK DON' YOU LIKE BASE-BALL?
S'BORING N'SHIT.
BORING? YOU EVER PLAY THE GAME?
DIDN' YOUR MAMA BUY YOU A MITT WHEN YOU WAS A BOY?
NAH, NOT REALLY ...COUPLE TIMES.
HERE. RUN THIS FROM THE POSITIVE TERMINAL TO THE COIL WIRE.
I DIDN' NEED NO MITT, POPS. NO ONE PLAYED BASEBALL IN THE HOOD. WE ALL SHOT HOOPS.

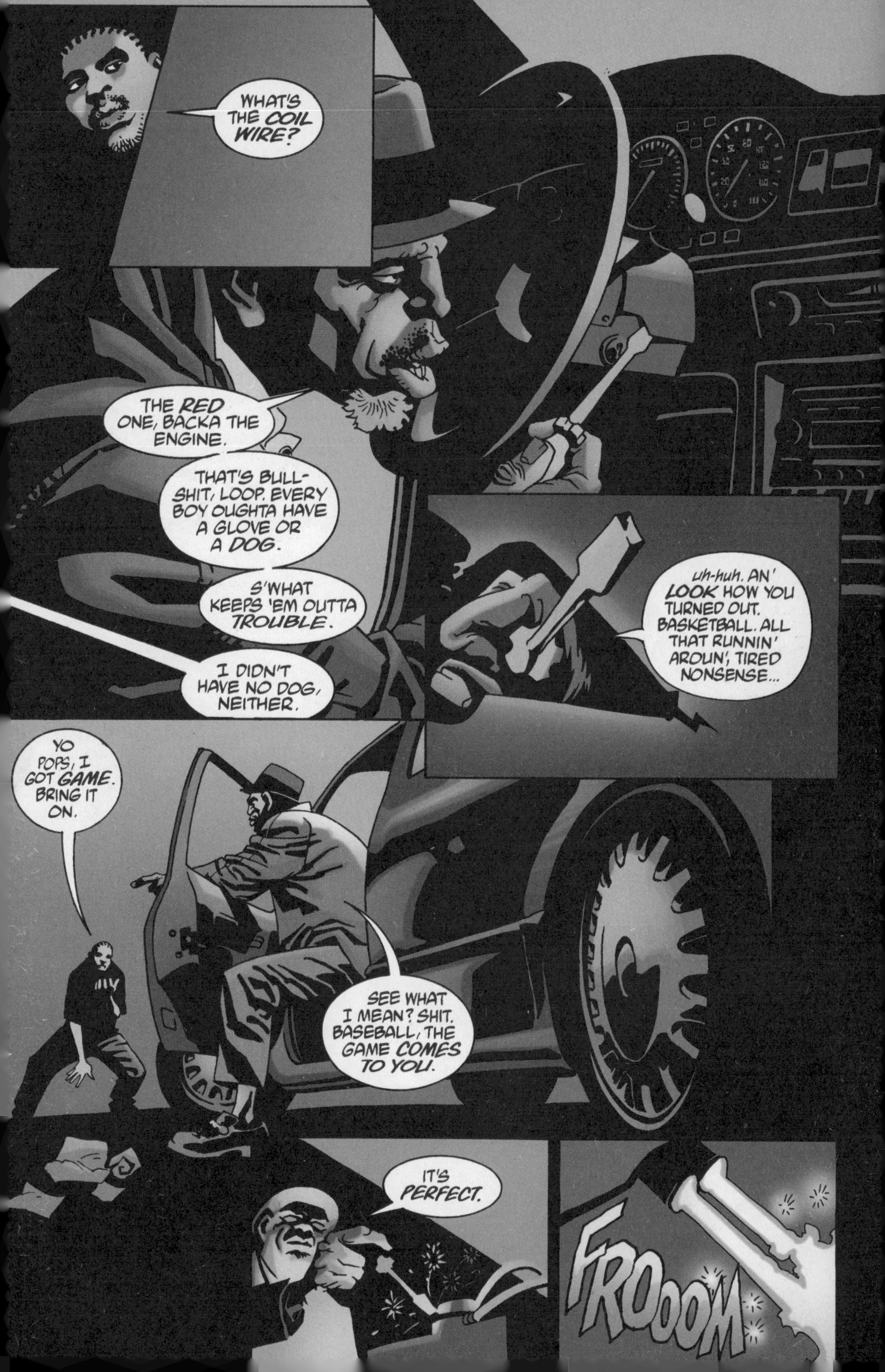
WHAT'S THE COIL WIRE?
THE RED ONE, BACKA THE ENGINE.
THAT'S BULL-SHIT, LOOP. EVERY BOY OUGHTA HAVE A GLOVE OR A DOG.
S'WHAT KEEPS 'EM OUTTA TROUBLE.
I DIDN'T HAVE NO DOG, NEITHER.
uh-huh. AN' LOOK HOW YOU TURNED OUT. BASKETBALL. ALL THAT RUNNIN' AROUN', TIRED NONSENSE...
YO POPS, I GOT GAME. BRING IT ON.
SEE WHAT I MEAN? SHIT. BASEBALL, THE GAME COMES TO YOU.
IT'S PERFECT.
FROOOM

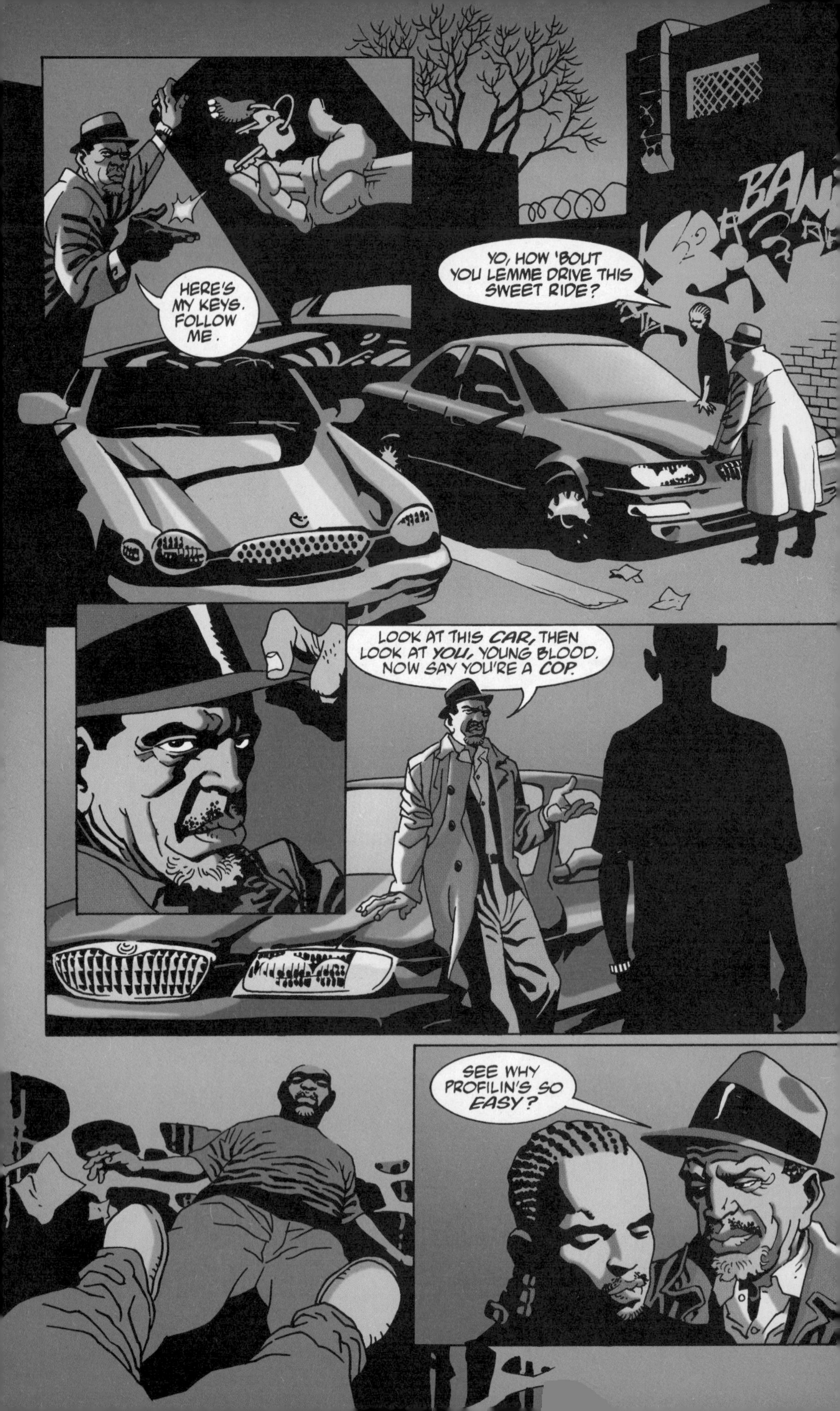
HERE'S MY KEYS. FOLLOW ME.
YO, HOW 'BOUT YOU LEMME DRIVE THIS SWEET RIDE?
LOOK AT THIS CAR, THEN LOOK AT YOU, YOUNG BLOOD. NOW SAY YOU'RE A COP.
SEE WHY PROFILIN'S SO EASY?

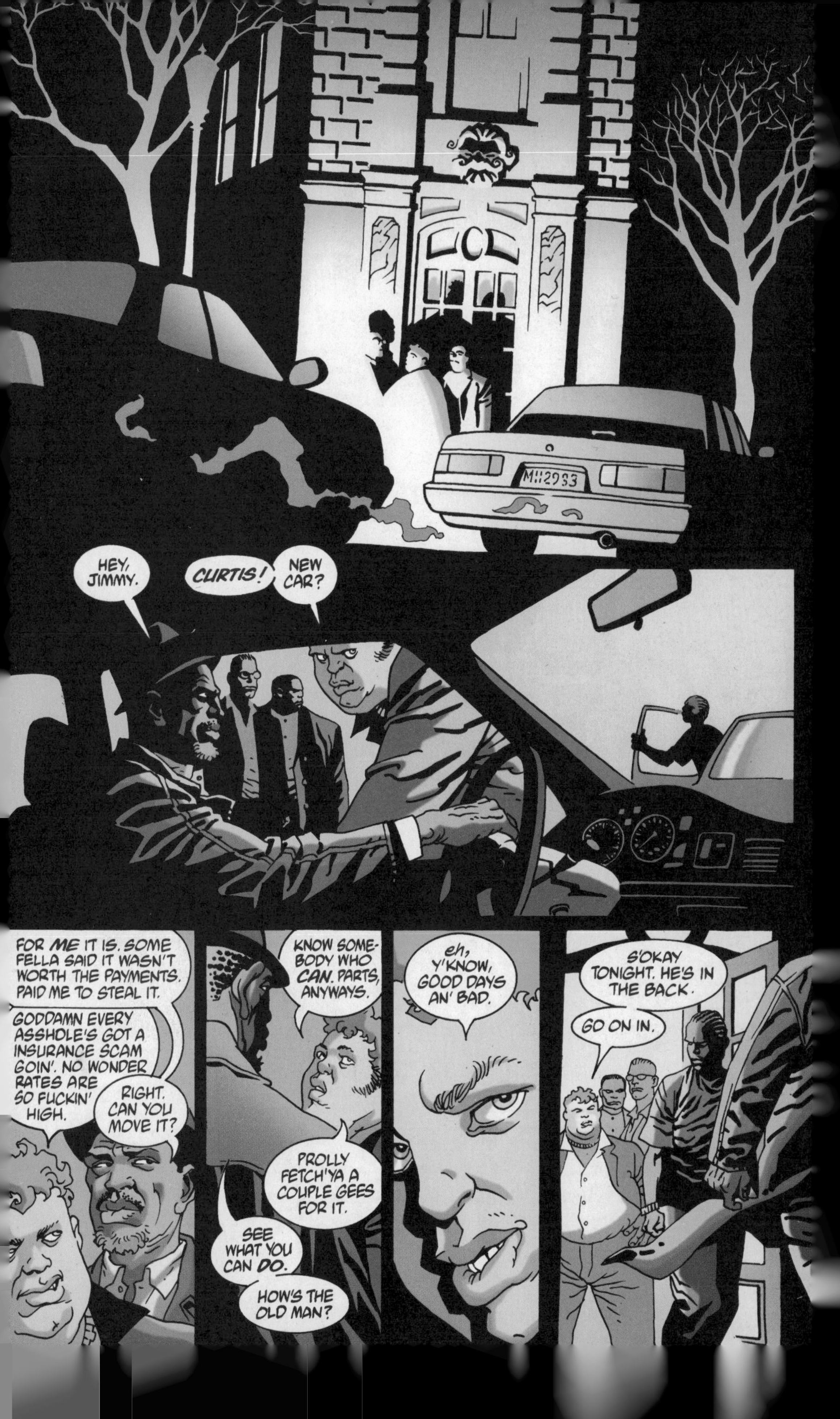
HEY, JIMMY.
CURTIS!
NEW CAR?
FOR ME IT IS. SOME FELLA SAID IT WASN'T WORTH THE PAYMENTS. PAID ME TO STEAL IT.
GODDAMN EVERY ASSHOLE'S GOT A INSURANCE SCAM GOIN'. NO WONDER RATES ARE SO FUCKIN' HIGH.
RIGHT. CAN YOU MOVE IT?
KNOW SOMEBODY WHO CAN. PARTS, ANYWAYS.
PROLLY FETCH'YA A COUPLE GEES FOR IT.
SEE WHAT YOU CAN DO.
HOW'S THE OLD MAN?
eh, Y'KNOW, GOOD DAYS AN' BAD.
S'OKAY TONIGHT. HE'S IN THE BACK.
GO ON IN.

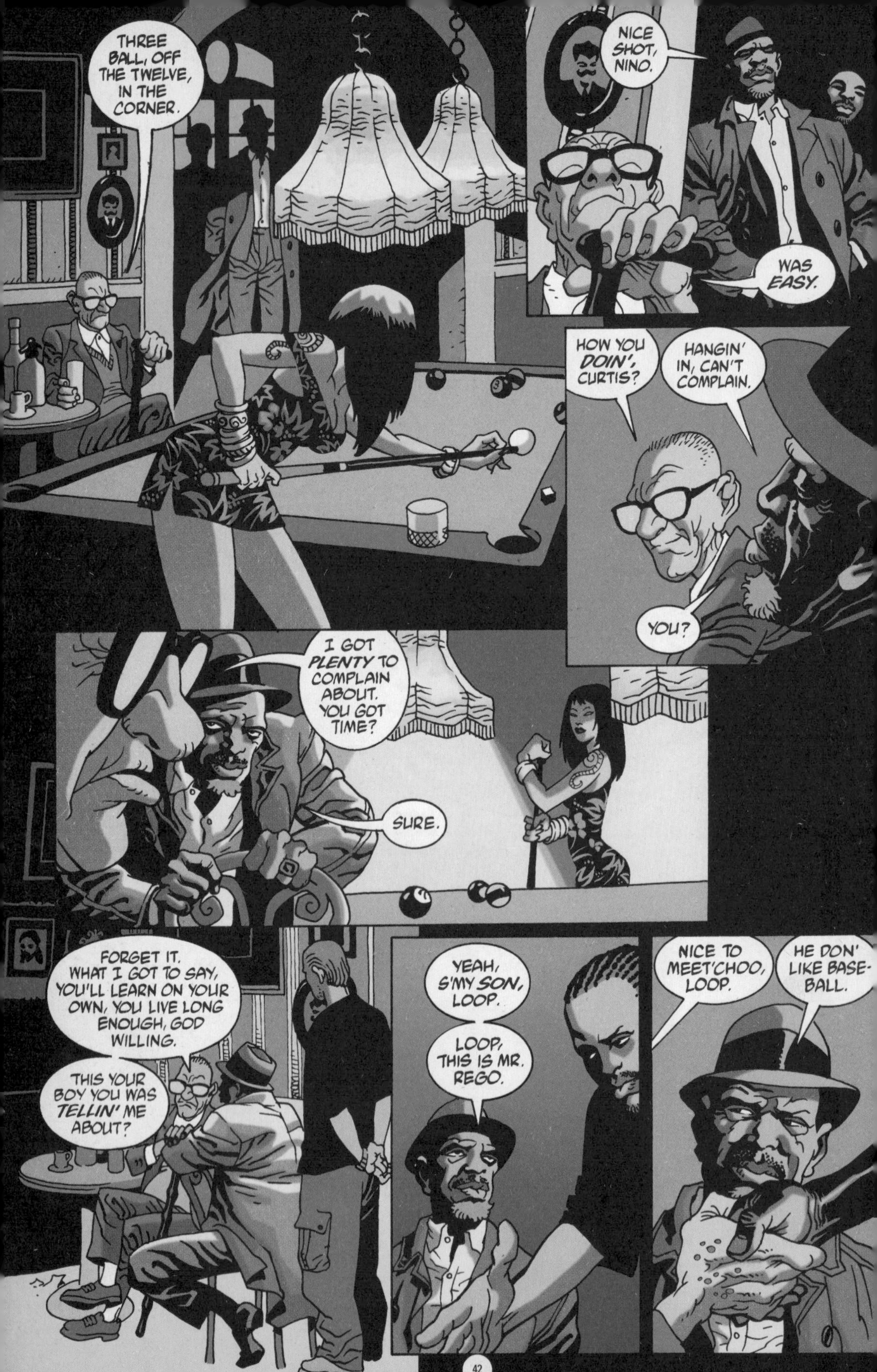
THREE BALL, OFF THE TWELVE, IN THE CORNER.
NICE SHOT, NINO.
WAS EASY.
HOW YOU DOIN', CURTIS?
HANGIN' IN, CAN'T COMPLAIN.
YOU?
I GOT PLENTY TO COMPLAIN ABOUT. YOU GOT TIME?
SURE.
FORGET IT. WHAT I GOT TO SAY, YOU'LL LEARN ON YOUR OWN, YOU LIVE LONG ENOUGH, GOD WILLING.
THIS YOUR BOY YOU WAS TELLIN' ME ABOUT?
YEAH, S'MY SON, LOOP.
LOOP, THIS IS MR. REGO.
NICE TO MEET'CHOO, LOOP.
HE DON' LIKE BASE-BALL.

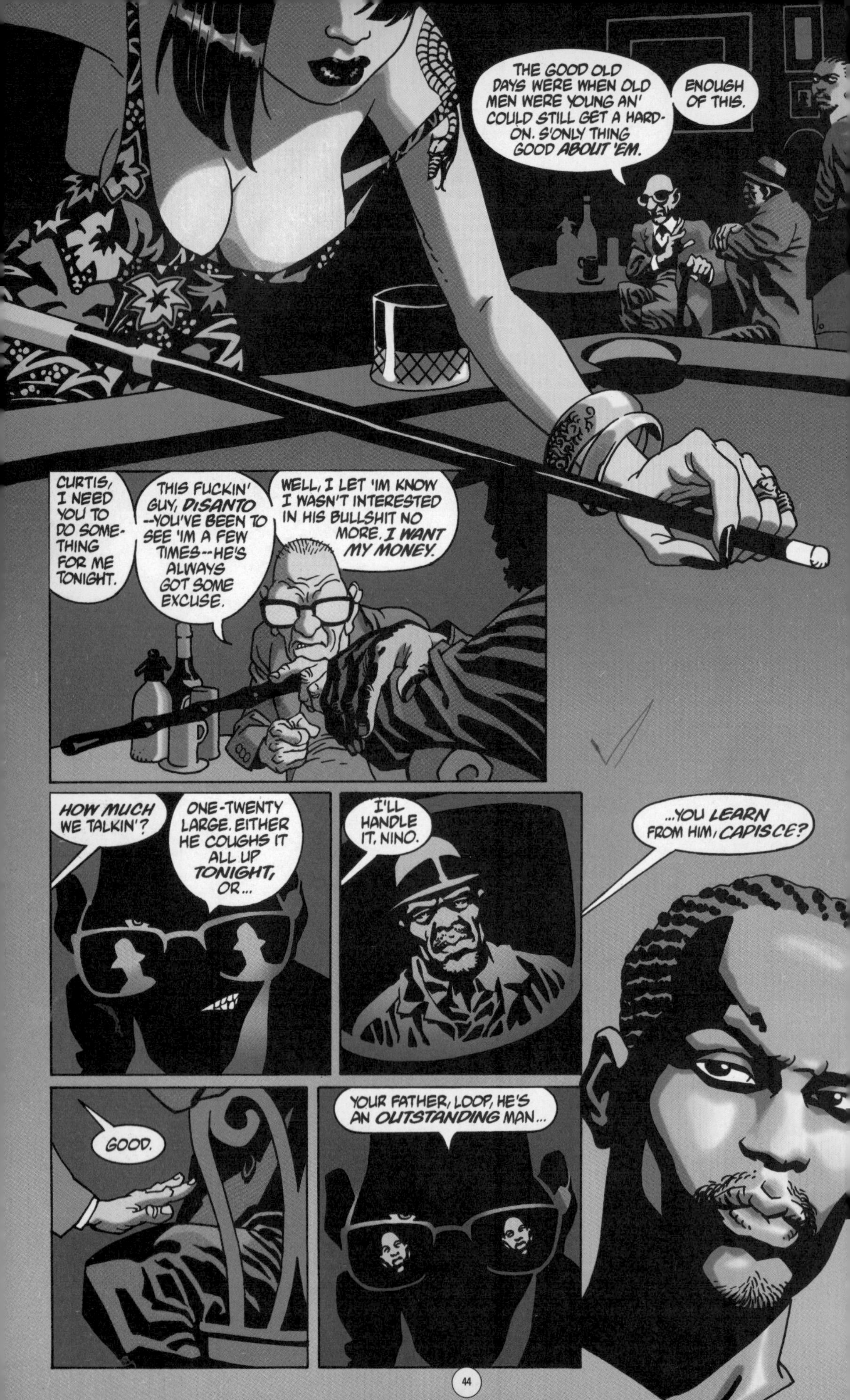
THE GOOD OLD DAYS WERE WHEN OLD MEN WERE YOUNG AN' COULD STILL GET A HARD-ON. S'ONLY THING GOOD ABOUT 'EM.
ENOUGH OF THIS.
CURTIS, I NEED YOU TO DO SOME-THING FOR ME TONIGHT.
THIS FUCKIN' GUY, DiSANTO --YOU'VE BEEN TO SEE 'IM A FEW TIMES--HE'S ALWAYS GOT SOME EXCUSE.
WELL, I LET 'IM KNOW I WASN'T INTERESTED IN HIS BULLSHIT NO MORE. I WANT MY MONEY.
HOW MUCH WE TALKIN'?
ONE-TWENTY LARGE. EITHER HE COUGHS IT ALL UP TONIGHT, OR...
I'LL HANDLE IT, NINO.
GOOD.
YOUR FATHER, LOOP, HE'S AN OUTSTANDING MAN...
...YOU LEARN FROM HIM, CAPISCE?

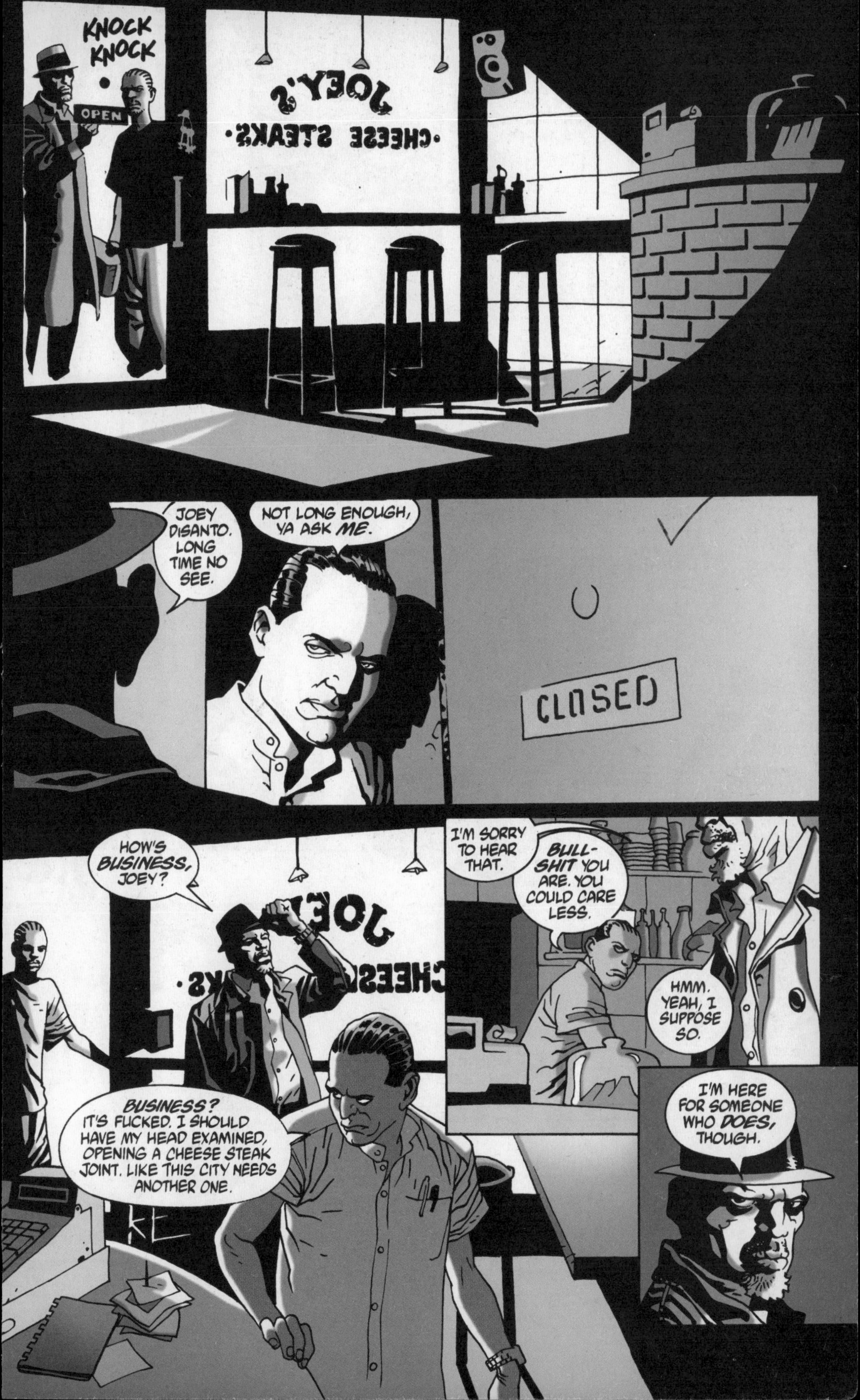
KNOCK KNOCK
OPEN
JOEY'S •CHEESE STEAKS•
JOEY DISANTO. LONG TIME NO SEE.
NOT LONG ENOUGH, YA ASK *ME*.
CLOSED
HOW'S *BUSINESS*, JOEY?
BUSINESS? IT'S FUCKED. I SHOULD HAVE MY HEAD EXAMINED, OPENING A CHEESE STEAK JOINT. LIKE THIS CITY NEEDS ANOTHER ONE.
I'M SORRY TO HEAR THAT.
BULL-SHIT YOU ARE. YOU COULD CARE LESS.
HMM. YEAH, I SUPPOSE SO.
I'M HERE FOR SOMEONE WHO *DOES*, THOUGH.

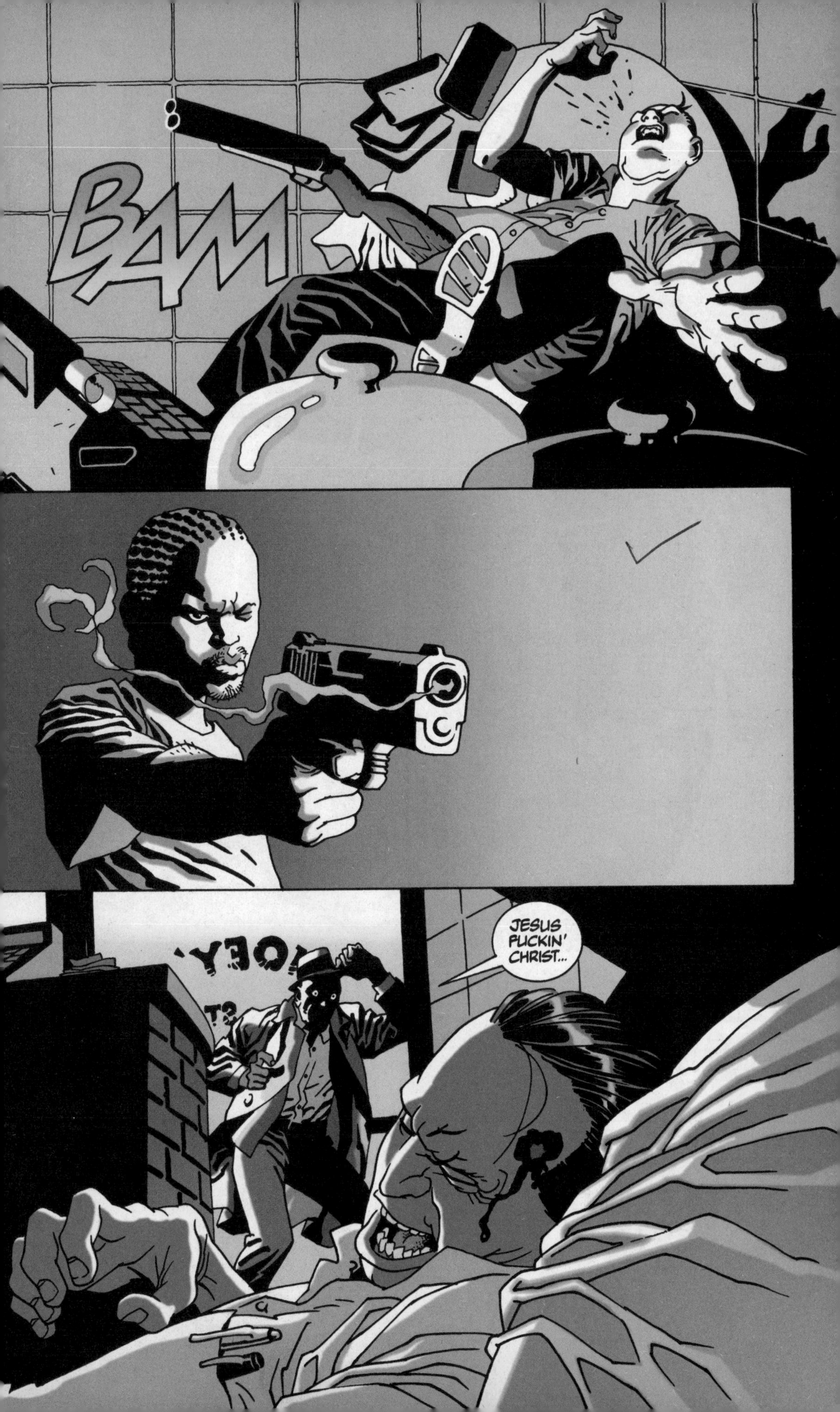
BAM
JESUS FUCKIN' CHRIST...

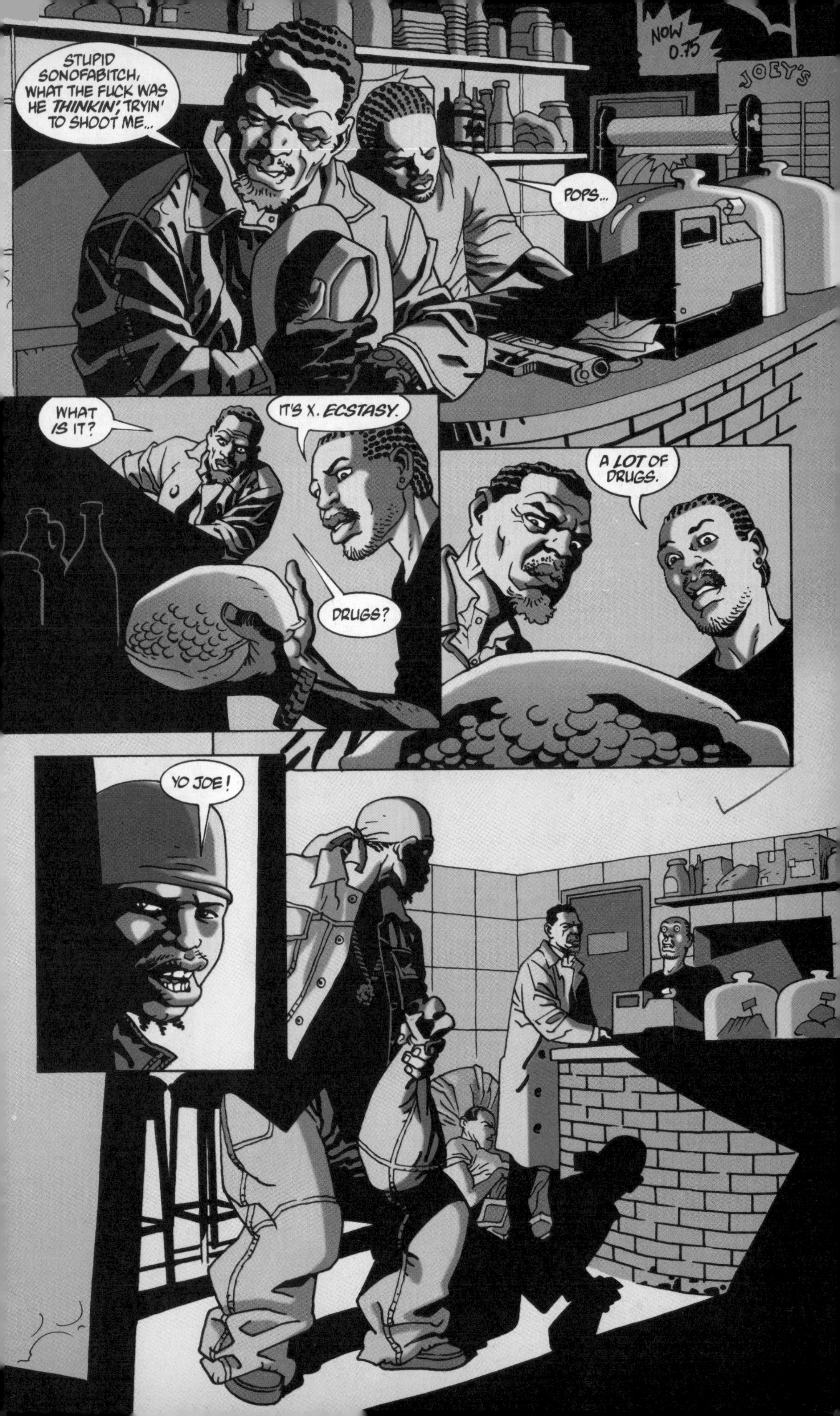
NOW 0.75
JOEY'S
STUPID SONOFABITCH, WHAT THE FUCK WAS HE *THINKIN'*, TRYIN' TO SHOOT ME...
POPS...
WHAT IS IT?
IT'S X. *ECSTASY.*
DRUGS?
A *LOT* OF DRUGS.
YO JOE!

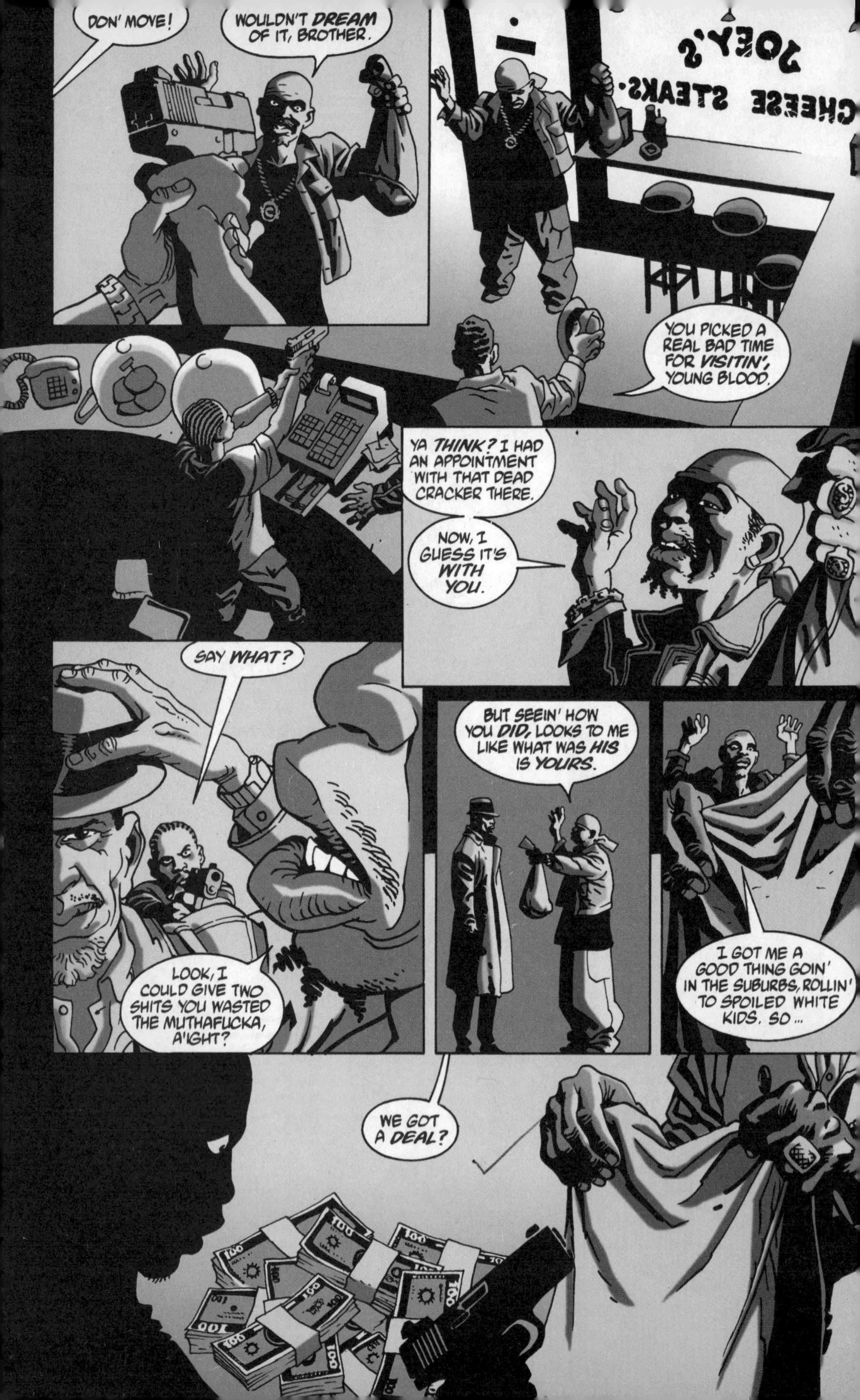
DON' MOVE!
WOULDN'T DREAM OF IT, BROTHER.
JOEY'S CHEESE STEAKS.
YOU PICKED A REAL BAD TIME FOR VISITIN', YOUNG BLOOD.
YA THINK? I HAD AN APPOINTMENT WITH THAT DEAD CRACKER THERE.
NOW, I GUESS IT'S WITH YOU.
SAY WHAT?
LOOK, I COULD GIVE TWO SHITS YOU WASTED THE MUTHAFUCKA, A'IGHT?
BUT SEEIN' HOW YOU DID, LOOKS TO ME LIKE WHAT WAS HIS IS YOURS.
I GOT ME A GOOD THING GOIN' IN THE SUBURBS, ROLLIN' TO SPOILED WHITE KIDS. SO ...
WE GOT A DEAL?

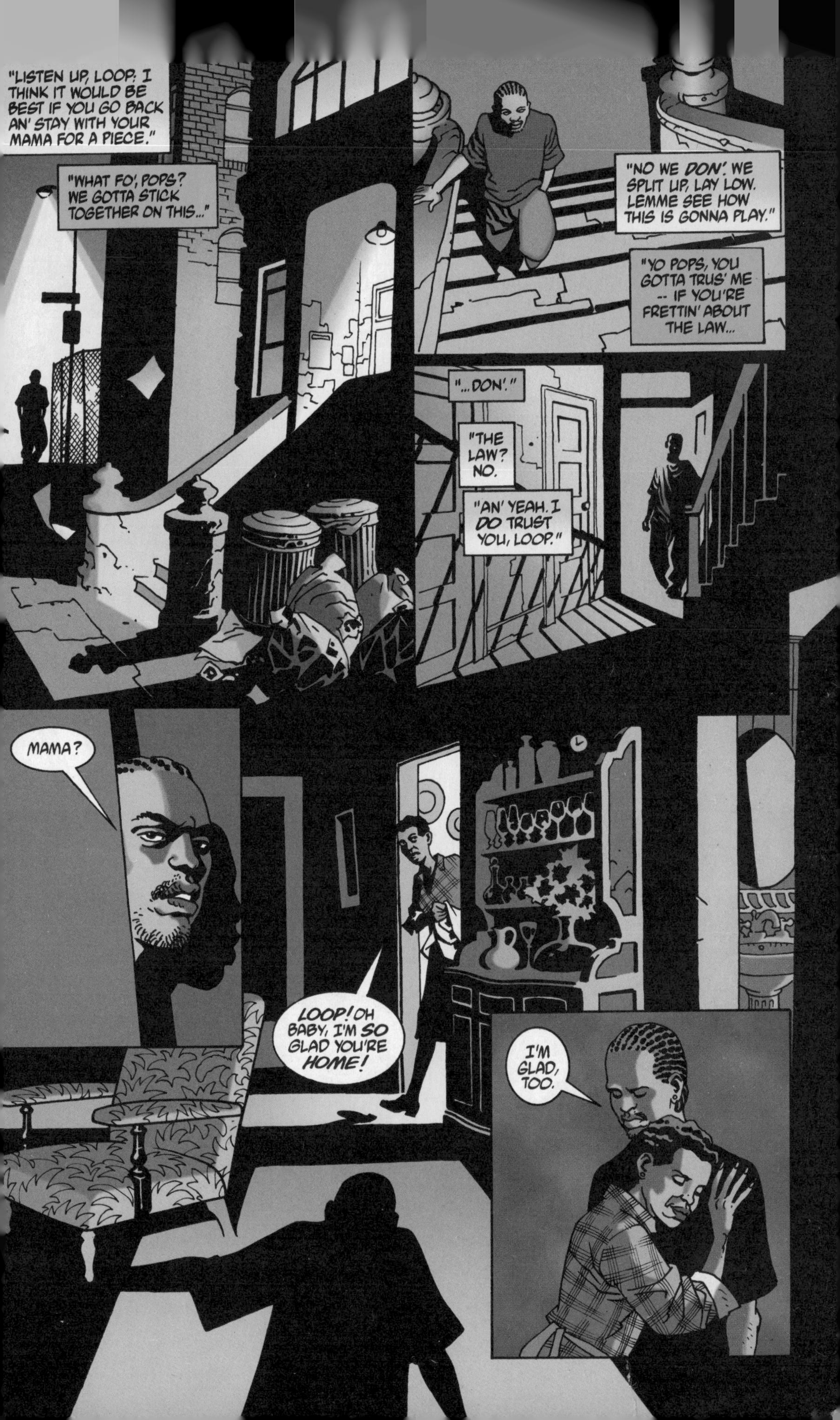
"LISTEN UP, LOOP: I THINK IT WOULD BE BEST IF YOU GO BACK AN' STAY WITH YOUR MAMA FOR A PIECE."
"WHAT FO', POPS? WE GOTTA STICK TOGETHER ON THIS..."
"NO WE DON'. WE SPLIT UP, LAY LOW. LEMME SEE HOW THIS IS GONNA PLAY."
"YO POPS, YOU GOTTA TRUS' ME -- IF YOU'RE FRETTIN' ABOUT THE LAW...
"...DON'."
"THE LAW? NO.
"AN' YEAH. I DO TRUST YOU, LOOP."
MAMA?
LOOP! OH BABY, I'M SO GLAD YOU'RE HOME!
I'M GLAD, TOO.

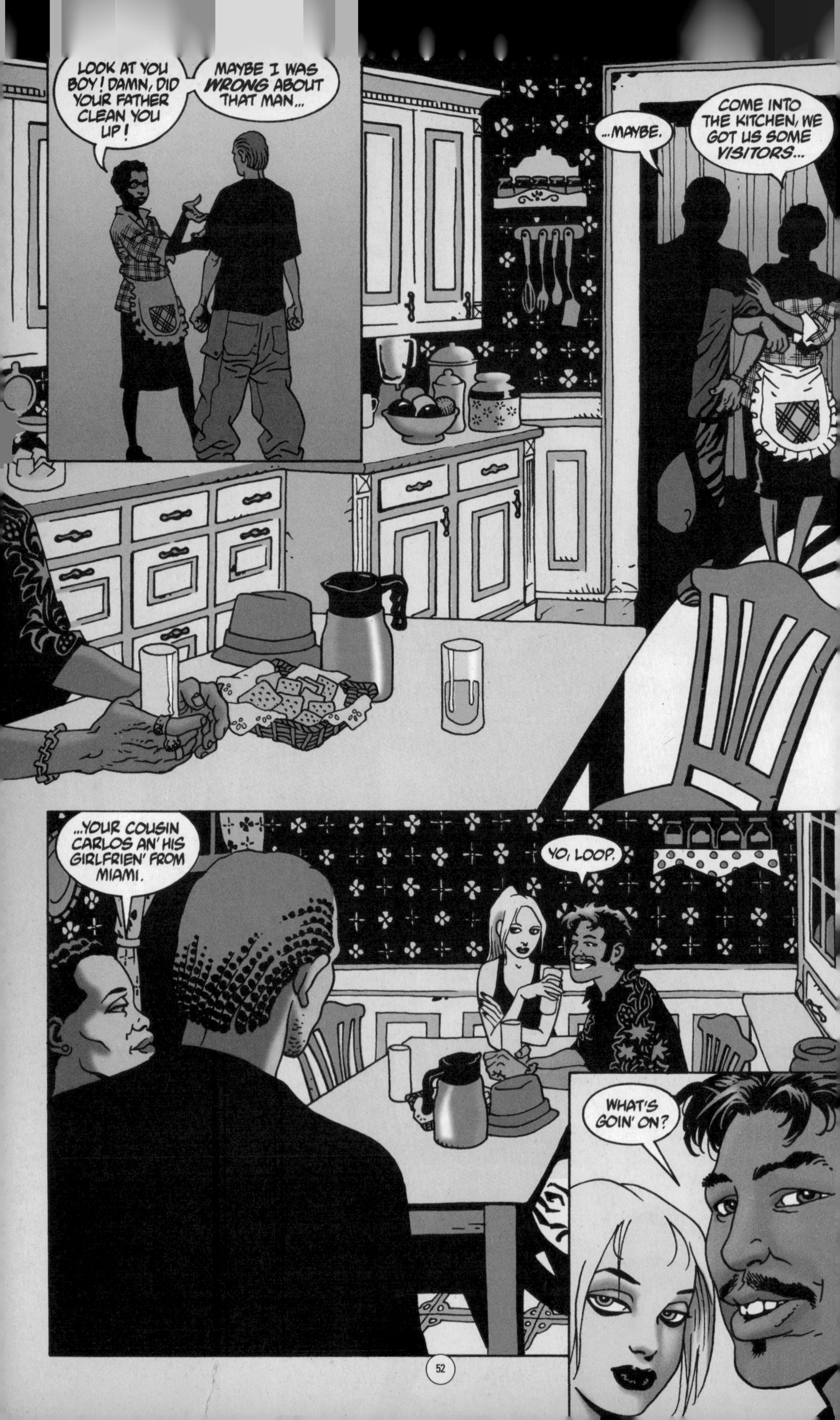
LOOK AT YOU BOY! DAMN, DID YOUR FATHER CLEAN YOU UP!
MAYBE I WAS **WRONG** ABOUT THAT MAN...
...MAYBE.
COME INTO THE KITCHEN, WE GOT US SOME *VISITORS*...
...YOUR COUSIN CARLOS AN' HIS GIRLFRIEN' FROM MIAMI.
YO, LOOP.
WHAT'S GOIN' ON?

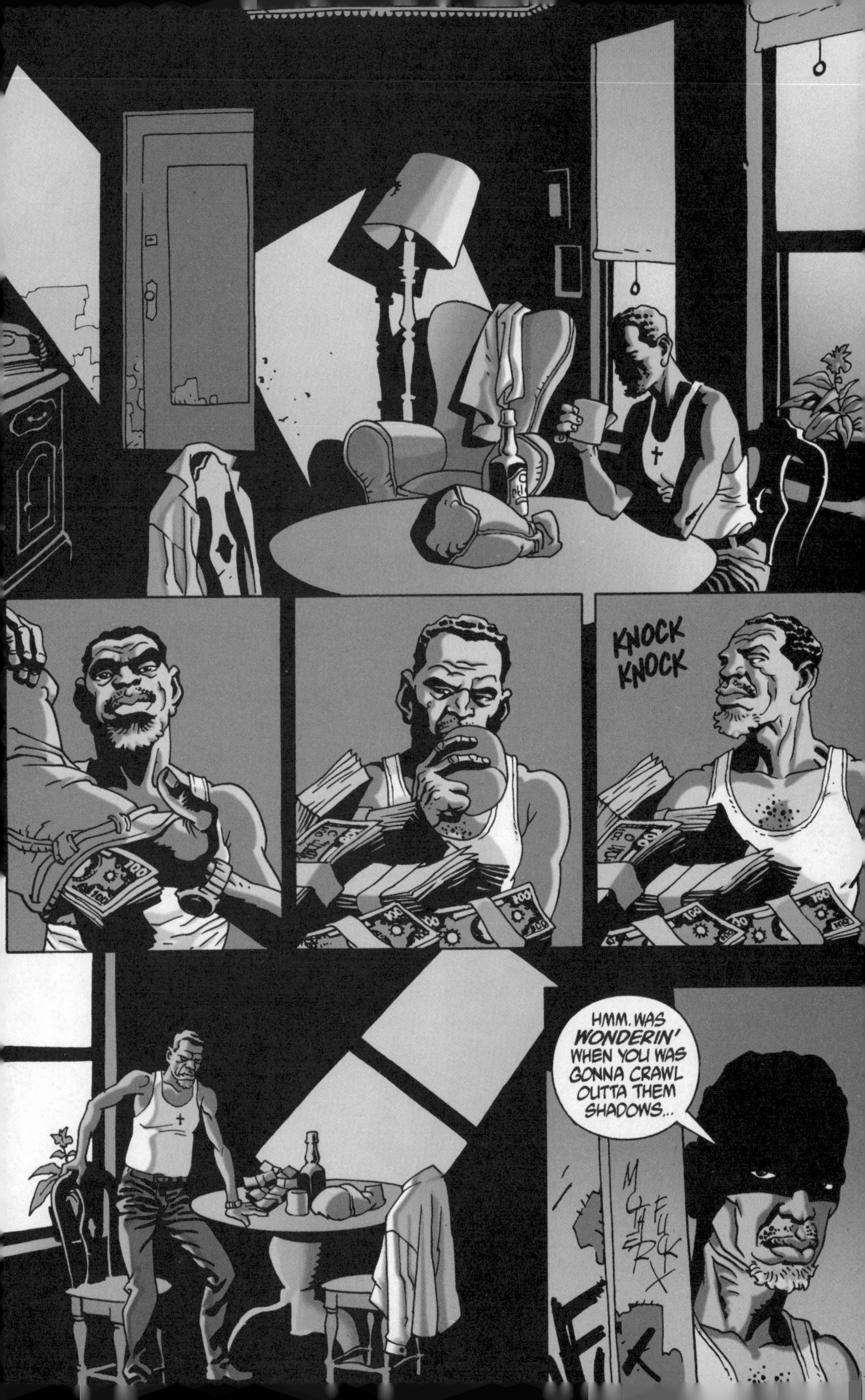
KNOCK KNOCK
HMM. WAS WONDERIN' WHEN YOU WAS GONNA CRAWL OUTTA THEM SHADOWS...

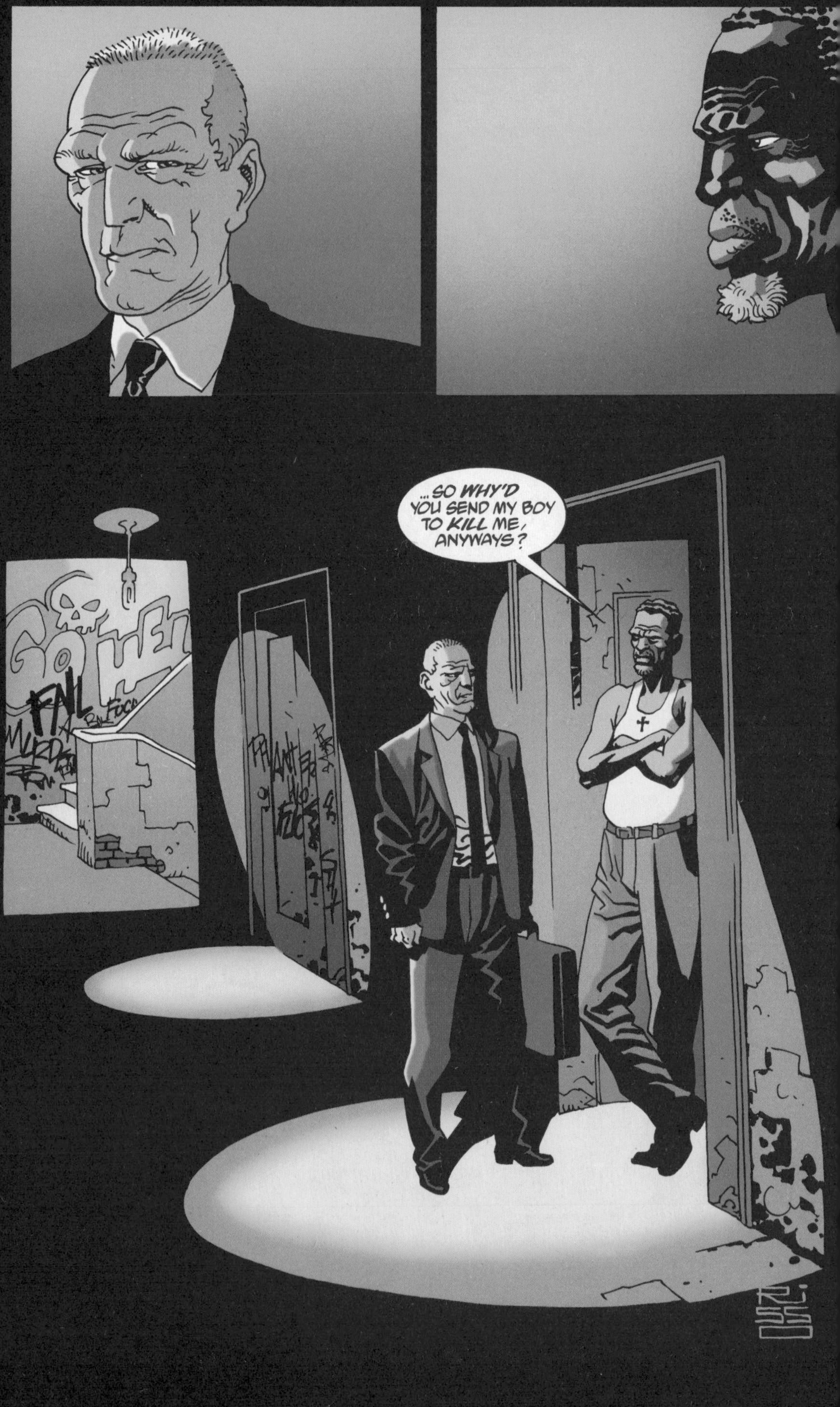
...SO WHY'D YOU SEND MY BOY TO KILL ME, ANYWAYS?

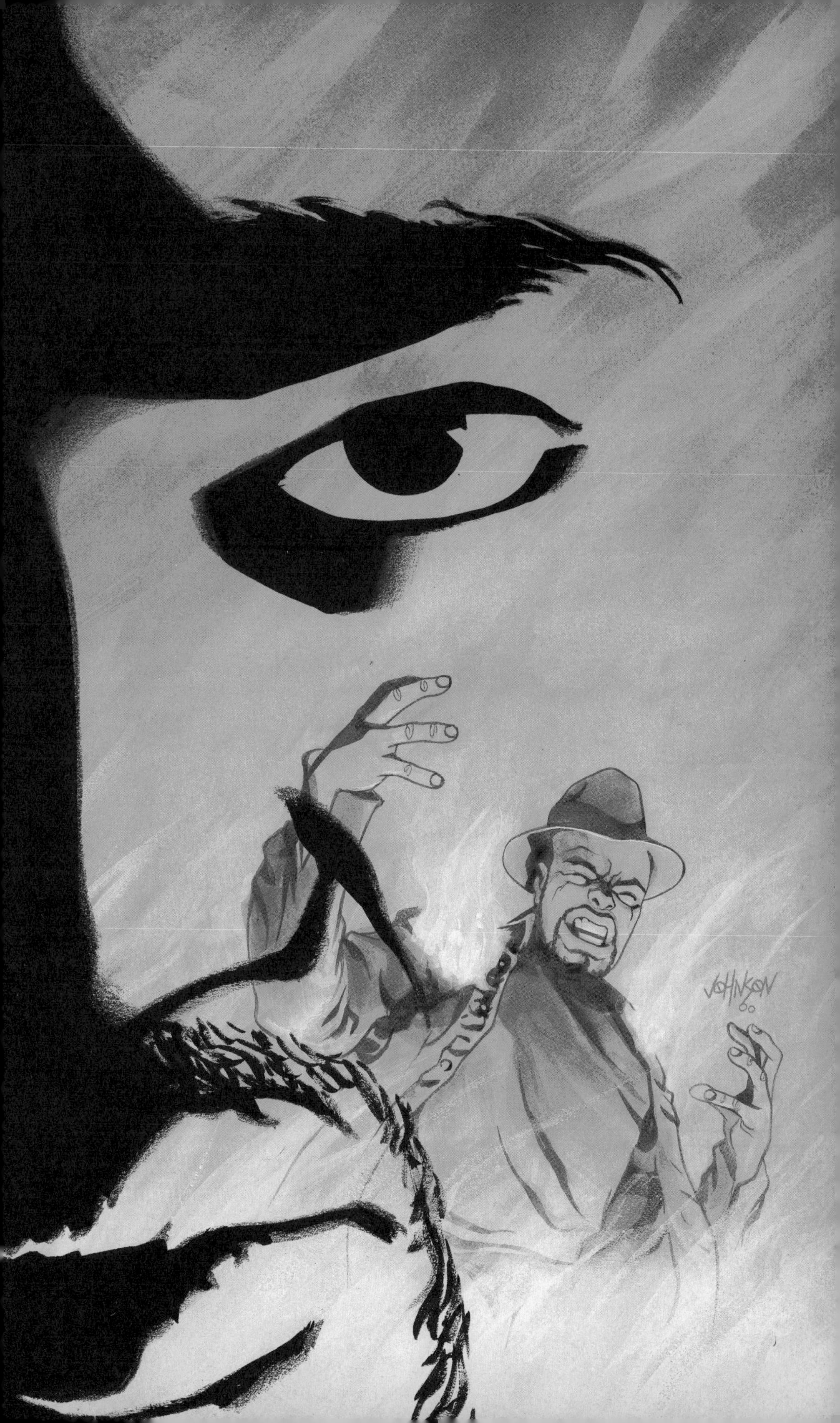
JOHNSON

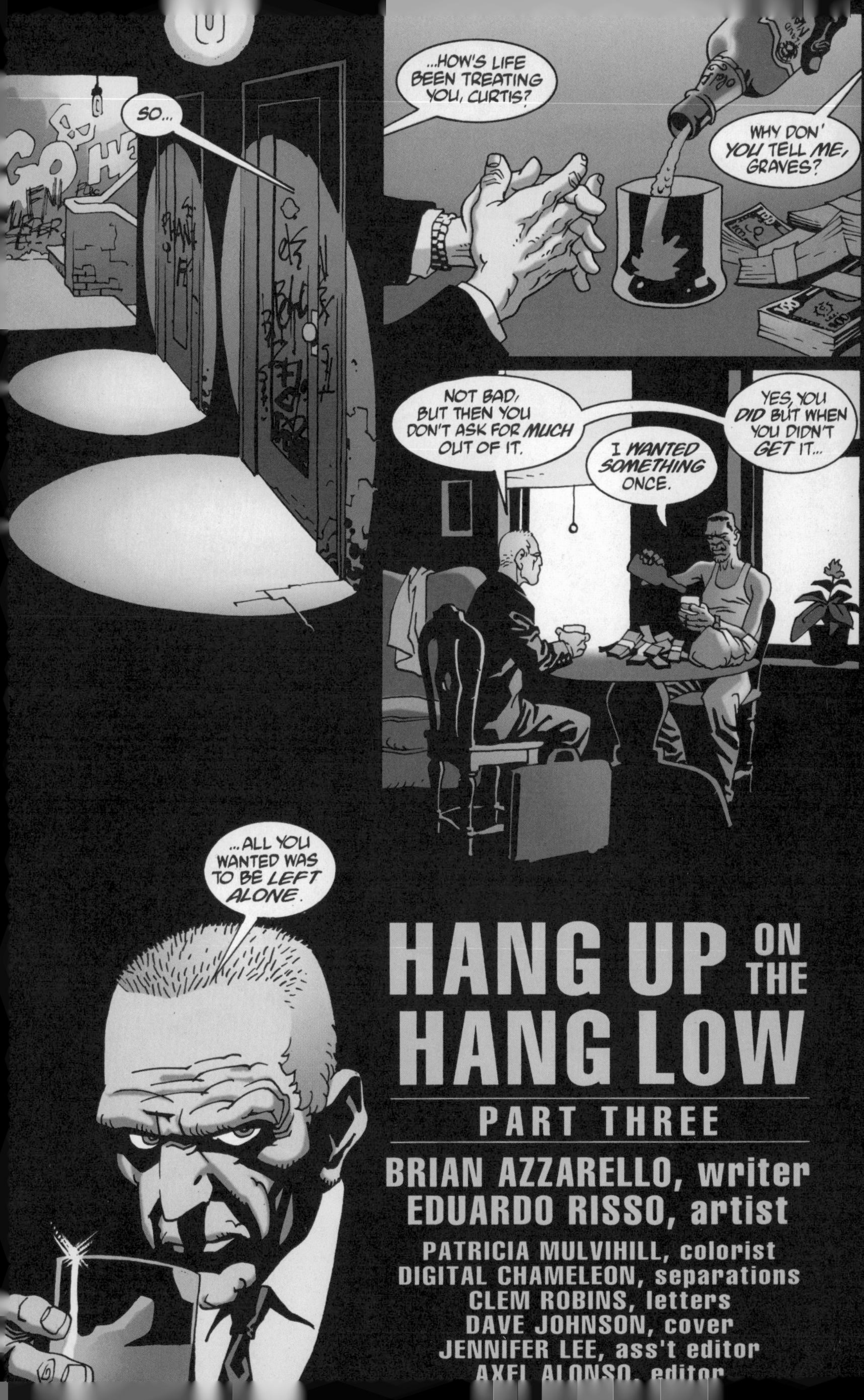
SO...
...HOW'S LIFE BEEN TREATING YOU, CURTIS?
WHY DON' YOU TELL ME, GRAVES?
NOT BAD, BUT THEN YOU DON'T ASK FOR MUCH OUT OF IT.
I WANTED SOMETHING ONCE.
YES, YOU DID BUT WHEN YOU DIDN'T GET IT...
...ALL YOU WANTED WAS TO BE LEFT ALONE.

HANG UP ON THE HANG LOW

PART THREE

BRIAN AZZARELLO, writer
EDUARDO RISSO, artist

PATRICIA MULVIHILL, colorist
DIGITAL CHAMELEON, separations
CLEM ROBINS, letters
DAVE JOHNSON, cover
JENNIFER LEE, ass't editor
AXEL ALONSO, editor

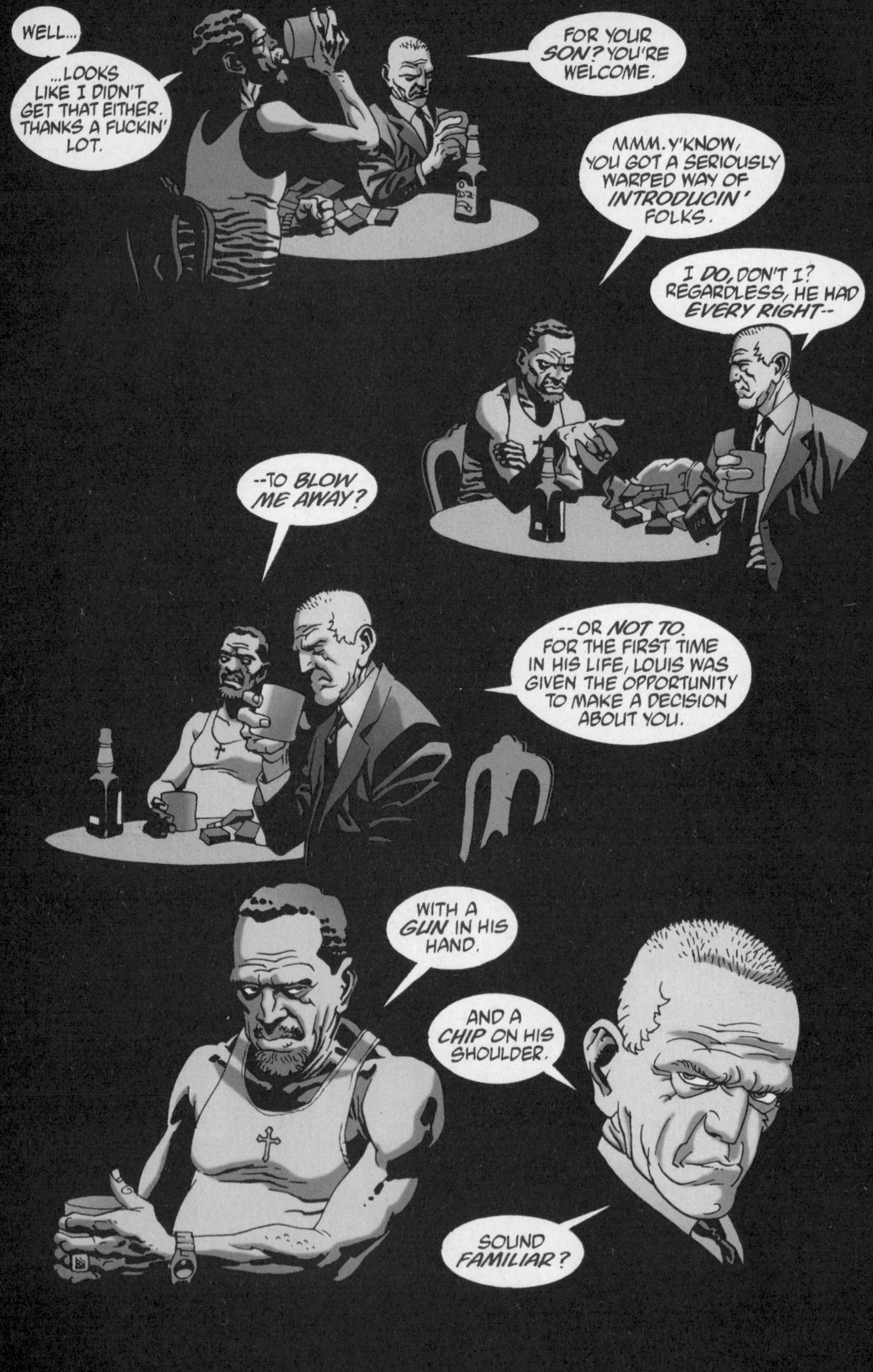
WELL...
...LOOKS LIKE I DIDN'T GET THAT EITHER. THANKS A FUCKIN' LOT.
FOR YOUR SON? YOU'RE WELCOME.
MMM. Y'KNOW, YOU GOT A SERIOUSLY WARPED WAY OF INTRODUCIN' FOLKS.
I DO, DON'T I? REGARDLESS, HE HAD EVERY RIGHT--
--TO BLOW ME AWAY?
--OR NOT TO. FOR THE FIRST TIME IN HIS LIFE, LOUIS WAS GIVEN THE OPPORTUNITY TO MAKE A DECISION ABOUT YOU.
WITH A GUN IN HIS HAND.
AND A CHIP ON HIS SHOULDER.
SOUND FAMILIAR?

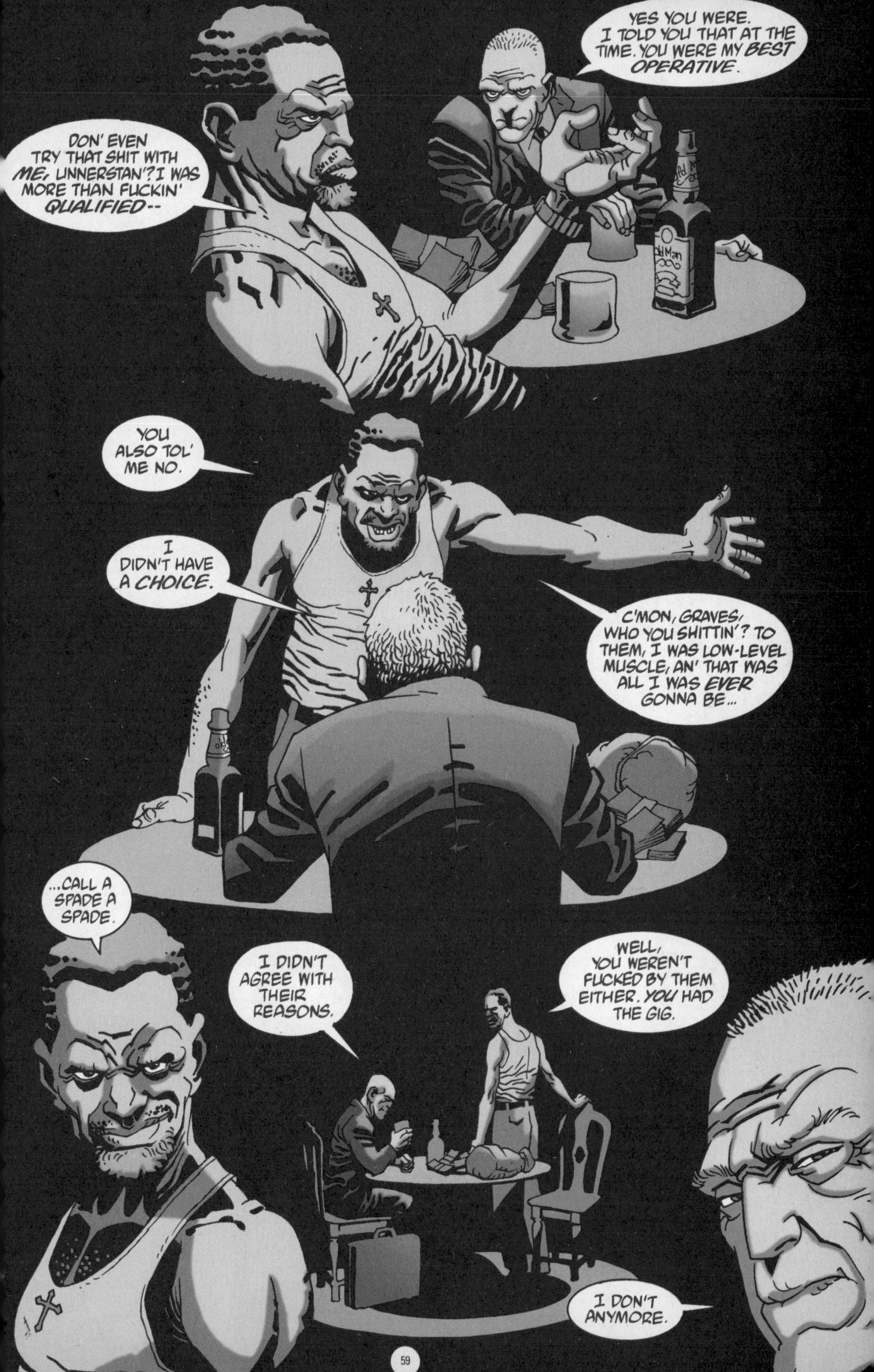
YES YOU WERE. I TOLD YOU THAT AT THE TIME. YOU WERE MY BEST OPERATIVE.
DON' EVEN TRY THAT SHIT WITH ME, UNNERSTAN'? I WAS MORE THAN FUCKIN' QUALIFIED--
YOU ALSO TOL' ME NO.
I DIDN'T HAVE A CHOICE.
C'MON, GRAVES, WHO YOU SHITTIN'? TO THEM, I WAS LOW-LEVEL MUSCLE, AN' THAT WAS ALL I WAS EVER GONNA BE...
...CALL A SPADE A SPADE.
I DIDN'T AGREE WITH THEIR REASONS.
WELL, YOU WEREN'T FUCKED BY THEM EITHER. YOU HAD THE GIG.
I DON'T ANYMORE.

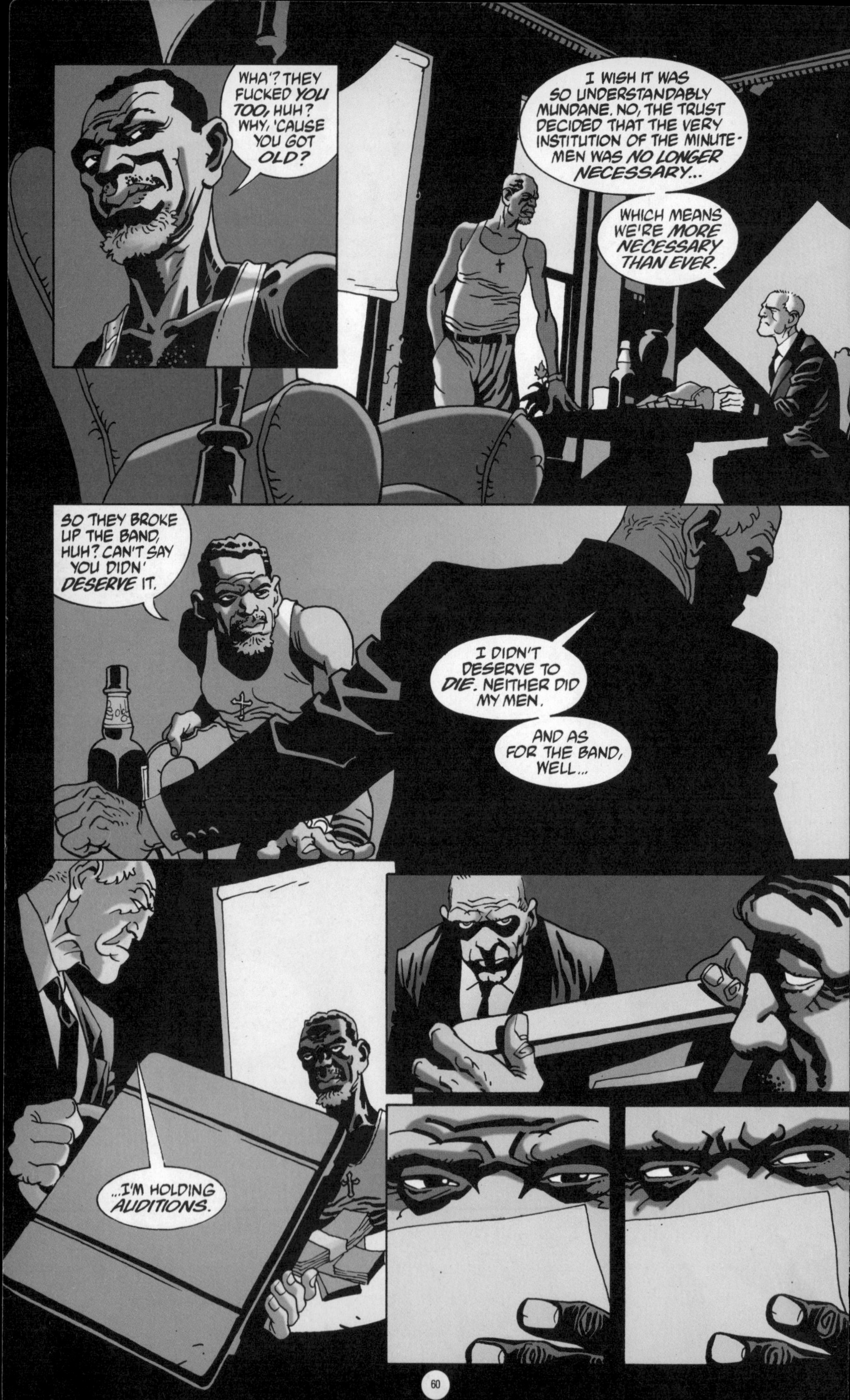

WHA'? THEY FUCKED YOU TOO, HUH? WHY, 'CAUSE YOU GOT OLD?
I WISH IT WAS SO UNDERSTANDABLY MUNDANE. NO, THE TRUST DECIDED THAT THE VERY INSTITUTION OF THE MINUTE-MEN WAS NO LONGER NECESSARY...
WHICH MEANS WE'RE MORE NECESSARY THAN EVER.
SO THEY BROKE UP THE BAND, HUH? CAN'T SAY YOU DIDN' DESERVE IT.
I DIDN'T DESERVE TO DIE. NEITHER DID MY MEN.
AND AS FOR THE BAND, WELL...
...I'M HOLDING AUDITIONS.

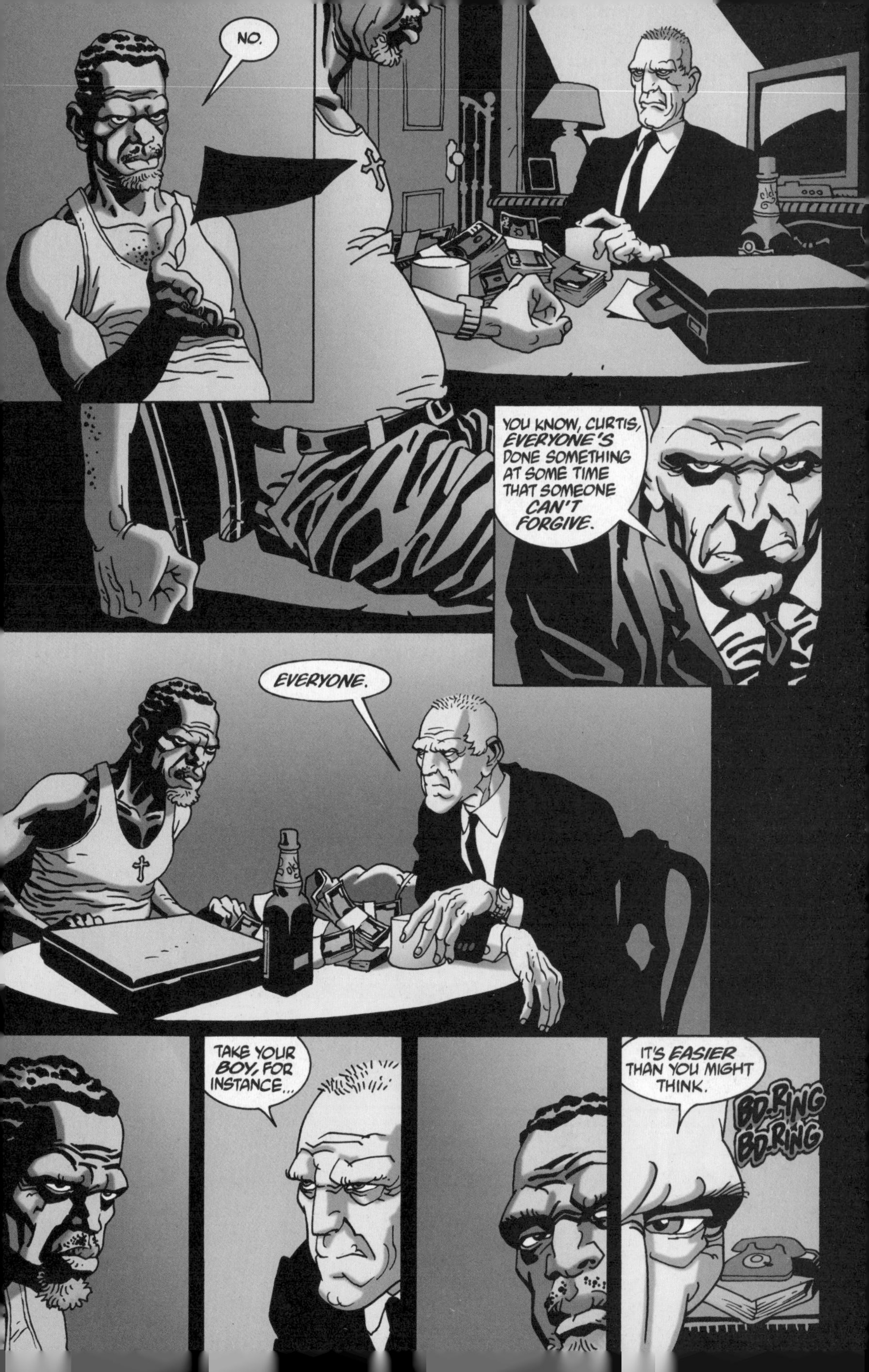
NO.
YOU KNOW, CURTIS, EVERYONE'S DONE SOMETHING AT SOME TIME THAT SOMEONE CAN'T FORGIVE.
EVERYONE.
TAKE YOUR BOY, FOR INSTANCE...
IT'S EASIER THAN YOU MIGHT THINK.
BD-RING
BD-RING

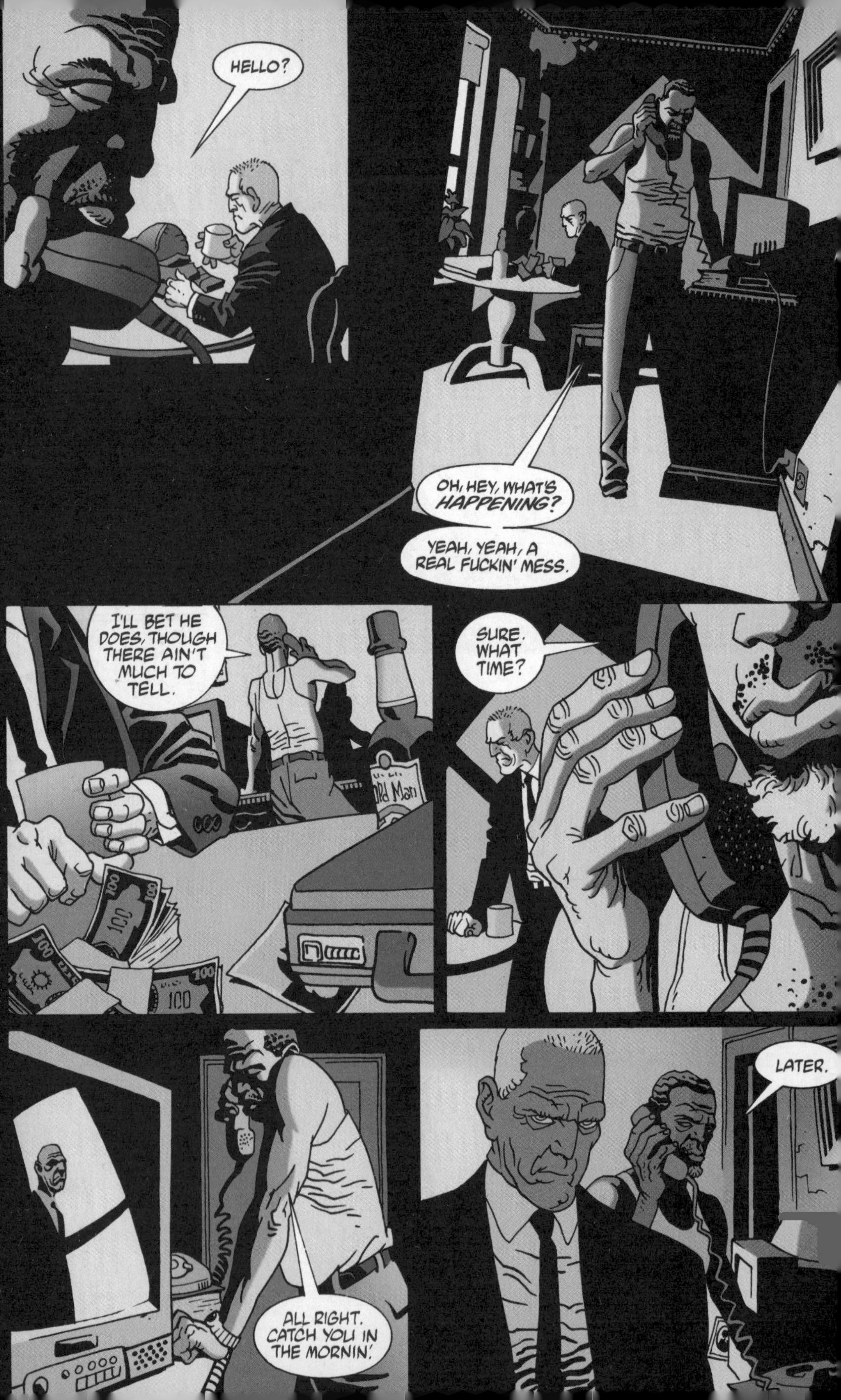
HELLO?
OH, HEY, WHAT'S HAPPENING?
YEAH, YEAH, A REAL FUCKIN' MESS.
I'LL BET HE DOES, THOUGH THERE AIN'T MUCH TO TELL.
SURE. WHAT TIME?
ALL RIGHT. CATCH YOU IN THE MORNIN'.
LATER.

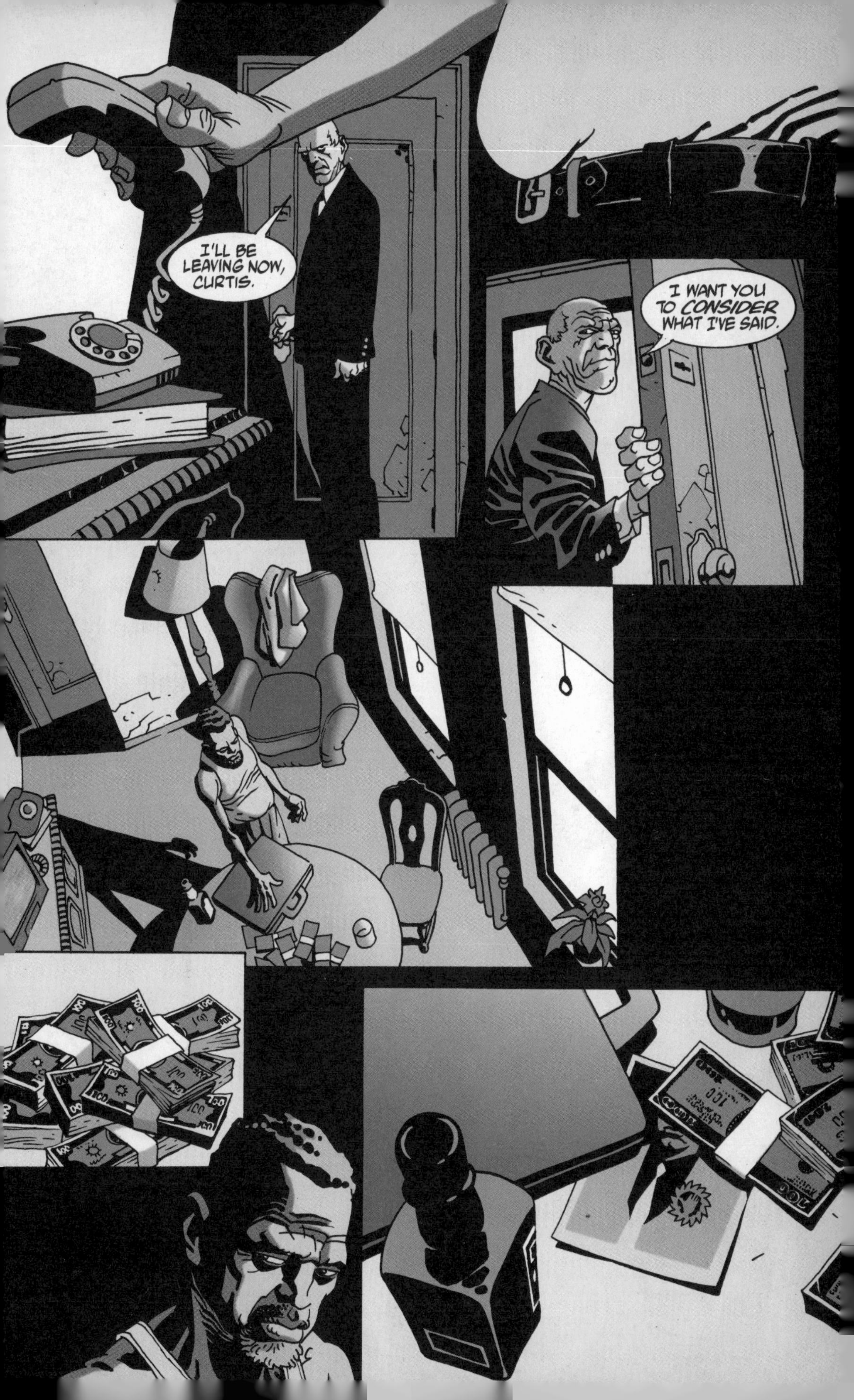
I'LL BE LEAVING NOW, CURTIS.
I WANT YOU TO CONSIDER WHAT I'VE SAID.

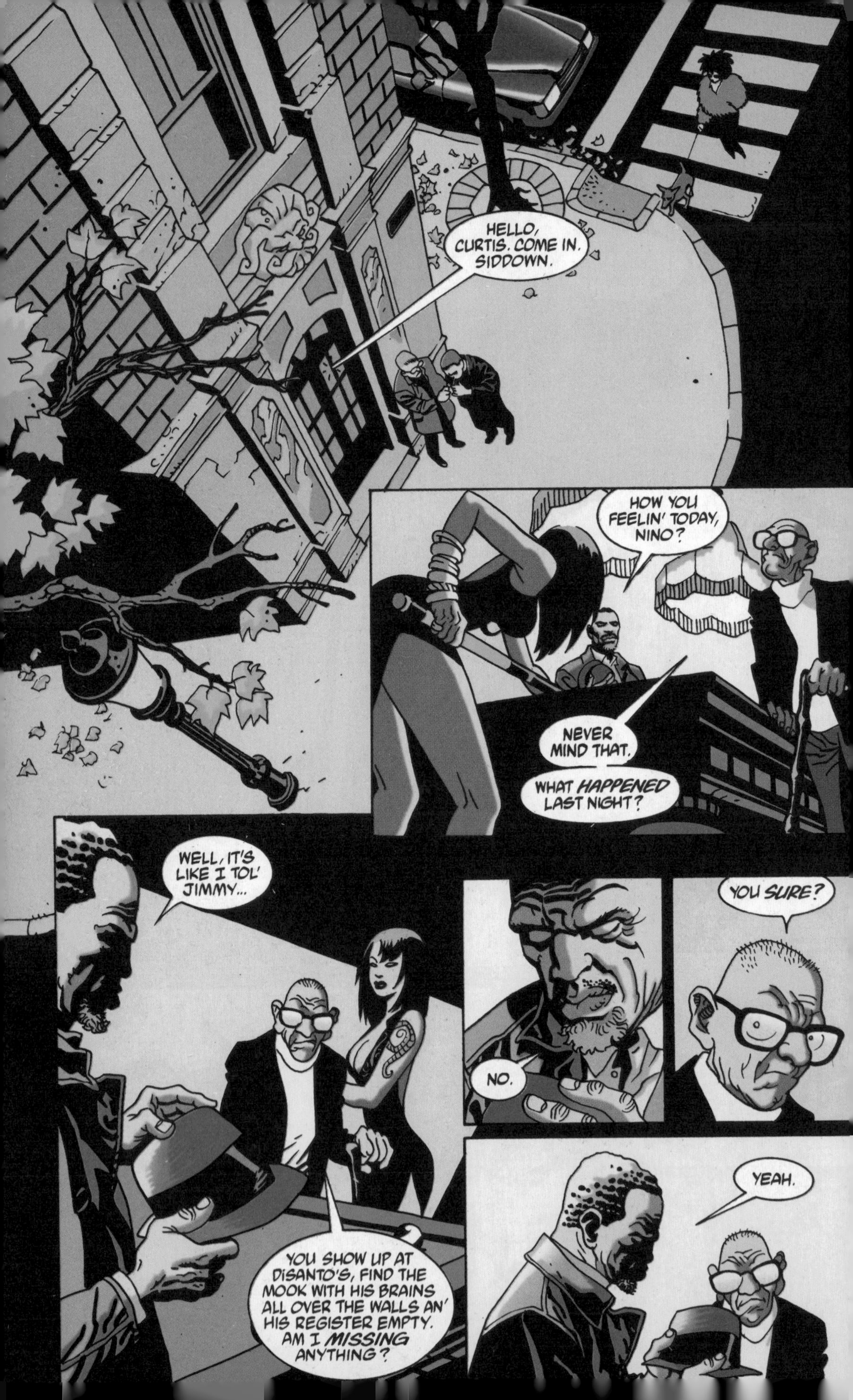
HELLO, CURTIS. COME IN. SIDDOWN.
HOW YOU FEELIN' TODAY, NINO?
NEVER MIND THAT.
WHAT HAPPENED LAST NIGHT?
WELL, IT'S LIKE I TOL' JIMMY...
YOU SHOW UP AT DiSANTO'S, FIND THE MOOK WITH HIS BRAINS ALL OVER THE WALLS AN' HIS REGISTER EMPTY. AM I MISSING ANYTHING?
NO.
YOU SURE?
YEAH.

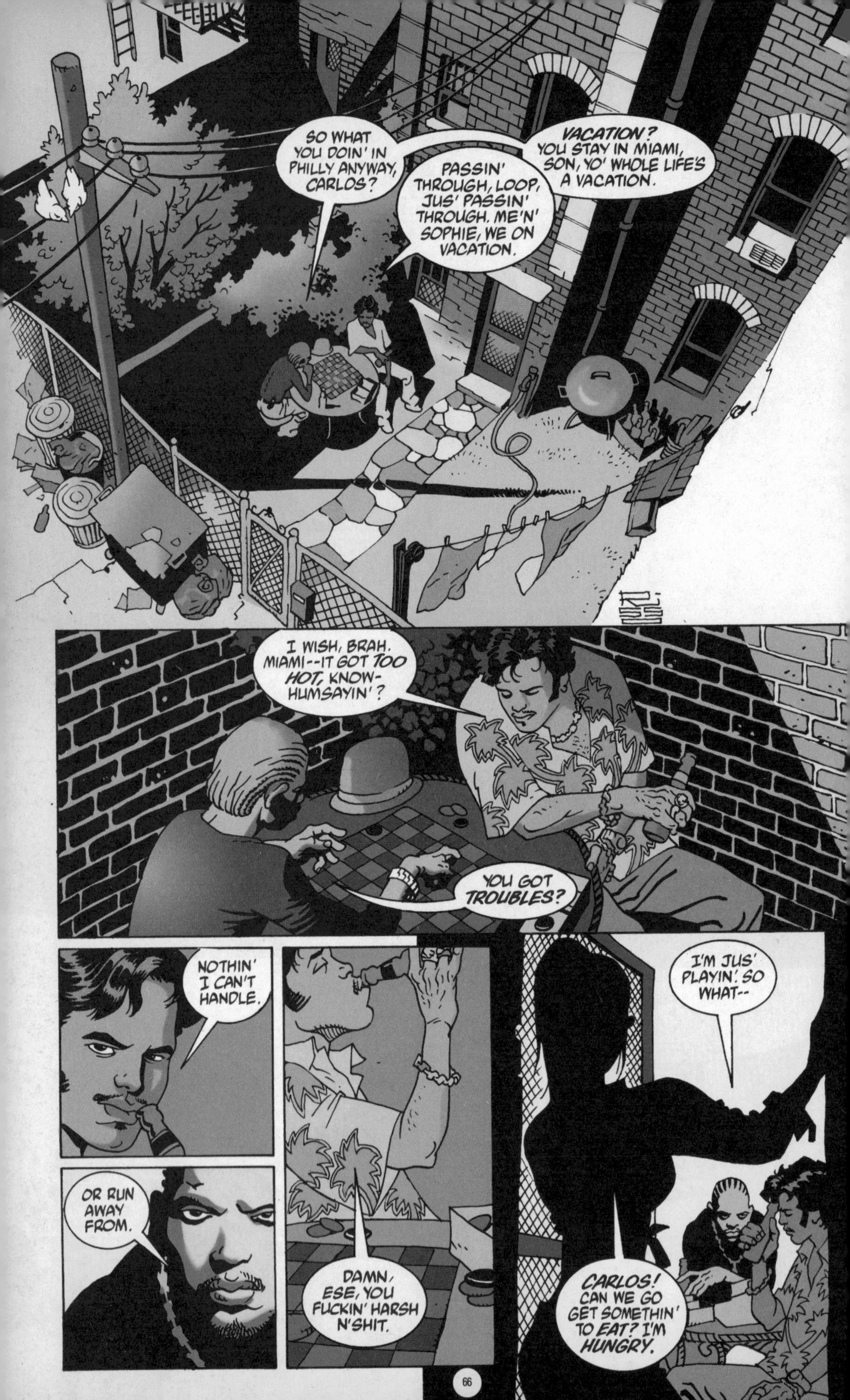
SO WHAT YOU DOIN' IN PHILLY ANYWAY, CARLOS?
PASSIN' THROUGH, LOOP, JUS' PASSIN' THROUGH. ME'N' SOPHIE, WE ON VACATION.
VACATION? YOU STAY IN MIAMI, SON, YO' WHOLE LIFE'S A VACATION.
I WISH, BRAH. MIAMI--IT GOT TOO HOT, KNOW-HUMSAYIN'?
YOU GOT TROUBLES?
NOTHIN' I CAN'T HANDLE.
OR RUN AWAY FROM.
DAMN, ESE, YOU FUCKIN' HARSH N'SHIT.
I'M JUS' PLAYIN'. SO WHAT--
CARLOS! CAN WE GO GET SOMETHIN' TO EAT? I'M HUNGRY.

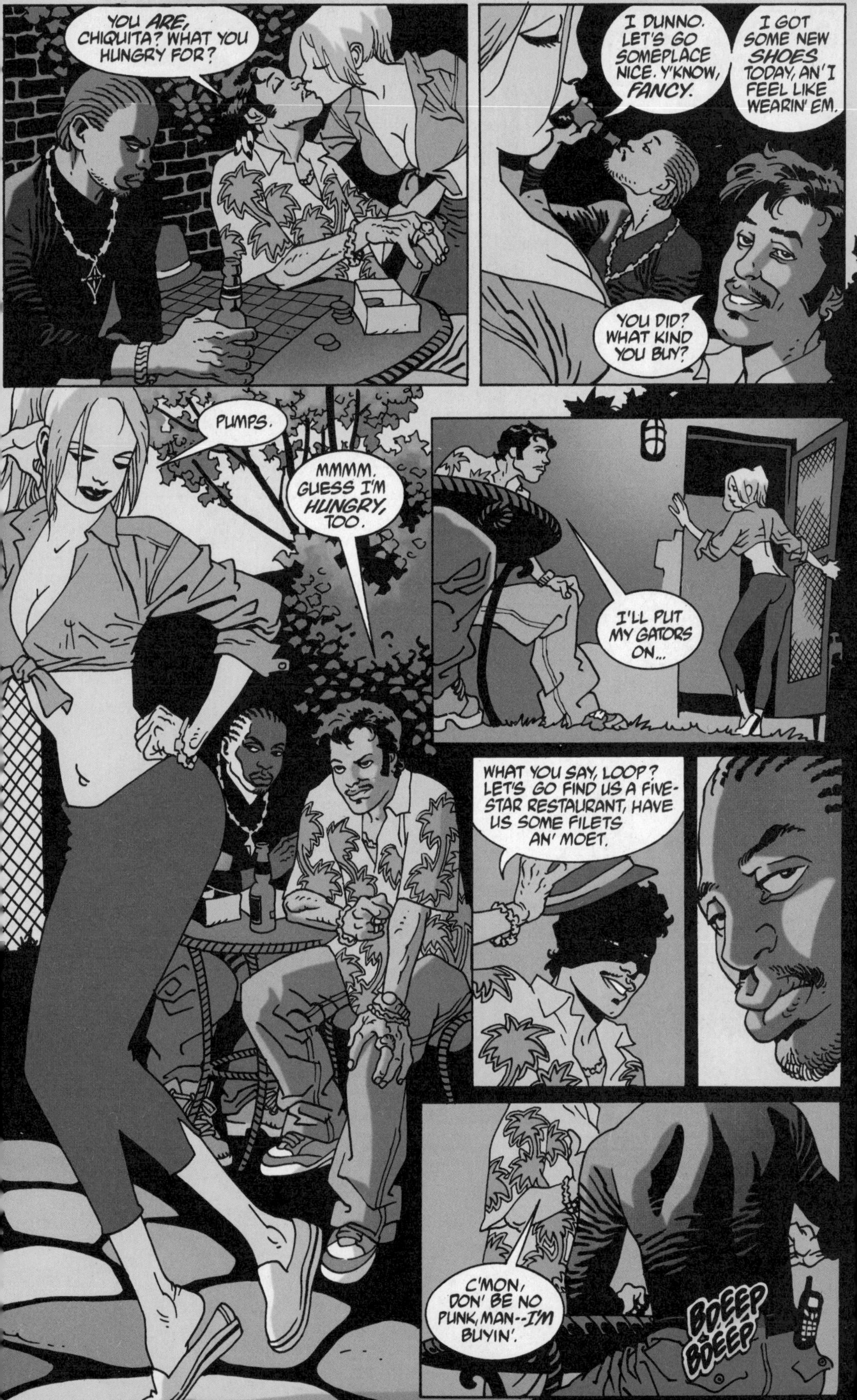
YOU ARE, CHIQUITA? WHAT YOU HUNGRY FOR?
I DUNNO. LET'S GO SOMEPLACE NICE. Y'KNOW, FANCY.
I GOT SOME NEW SHOES TODAY, AN' I FEEL LIKE WEARIN' EM.
YOU DID? WHAT KIND YOU BUY?
PUMPS.
MMMM. GUESS I'M HUNGRY, TOO.
I'LL PUT MY GATORS ON...
WHAT YOU SAY, LOOP? LET'S GO FIND US A FIVE-STAR RESTAURANT, HAVE US SOME FILETS AN' MOET.
C'MON, DON' BE NO PUNK, MAN--I'M BUYIN'.
BDEEP BDEEP

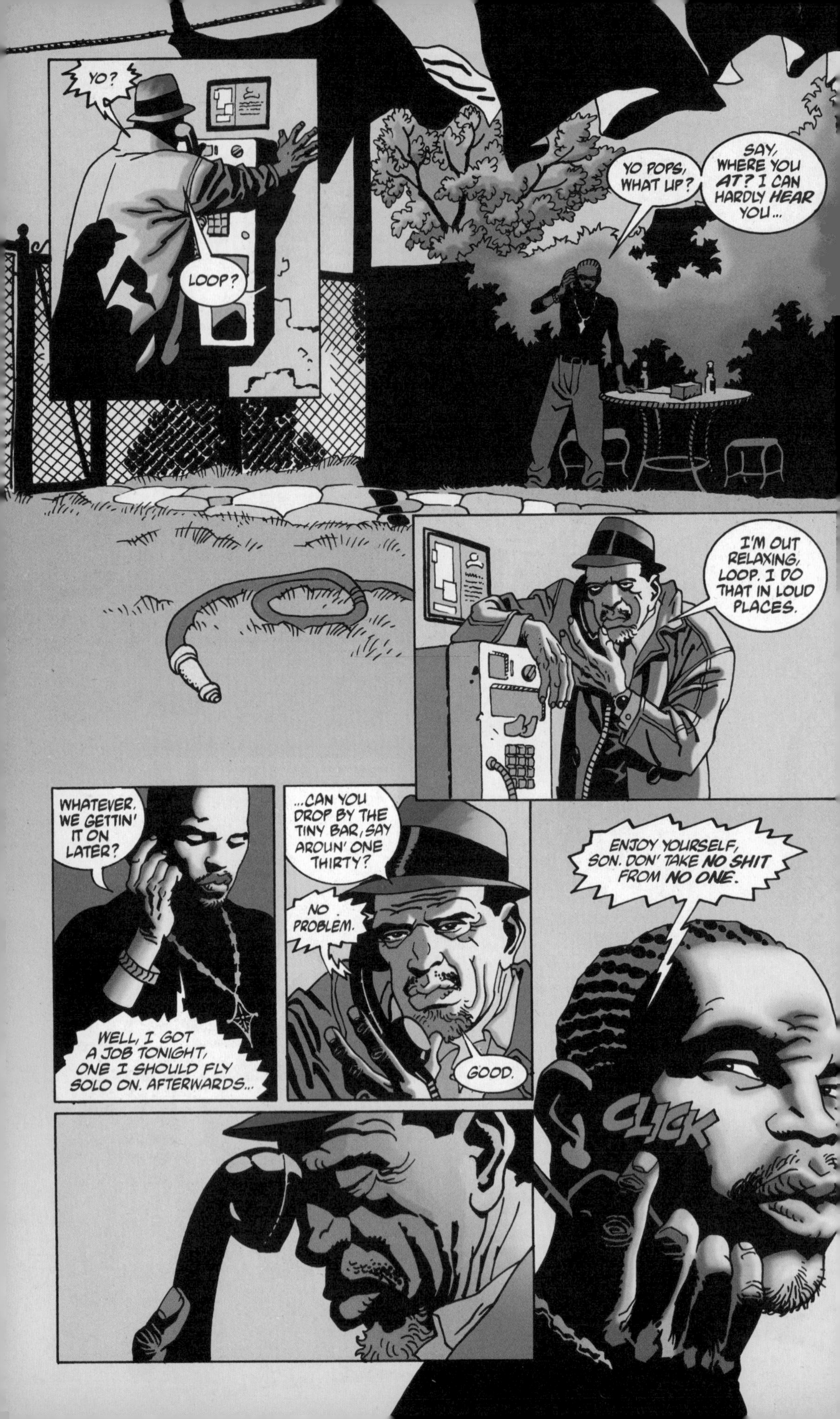
YO?
LOOP?
YO POPS, WHAT UP?
SAY, WHERE YOU AT? I CAN HARDLY HEAR YOU...
I'M OUT RELAXING, LOOP. I DO THAT IN LOUD PLACES.
WHATEVER. WE GETTIN' IT ON LATER?
WELL, I GOT A JOB TONIGHT, ONE I SHOULD FLY SOLO ON. AFTERWARDS...
...CAN YOU DROP BY THE TINY BAR, SAY AROUN' ONE THIRTY?
NO PROBLEM.
GOOD.
ENJOY YOURSELF, SON. DON' TAKE NO SHIT FROM NO ONE.
CLICK

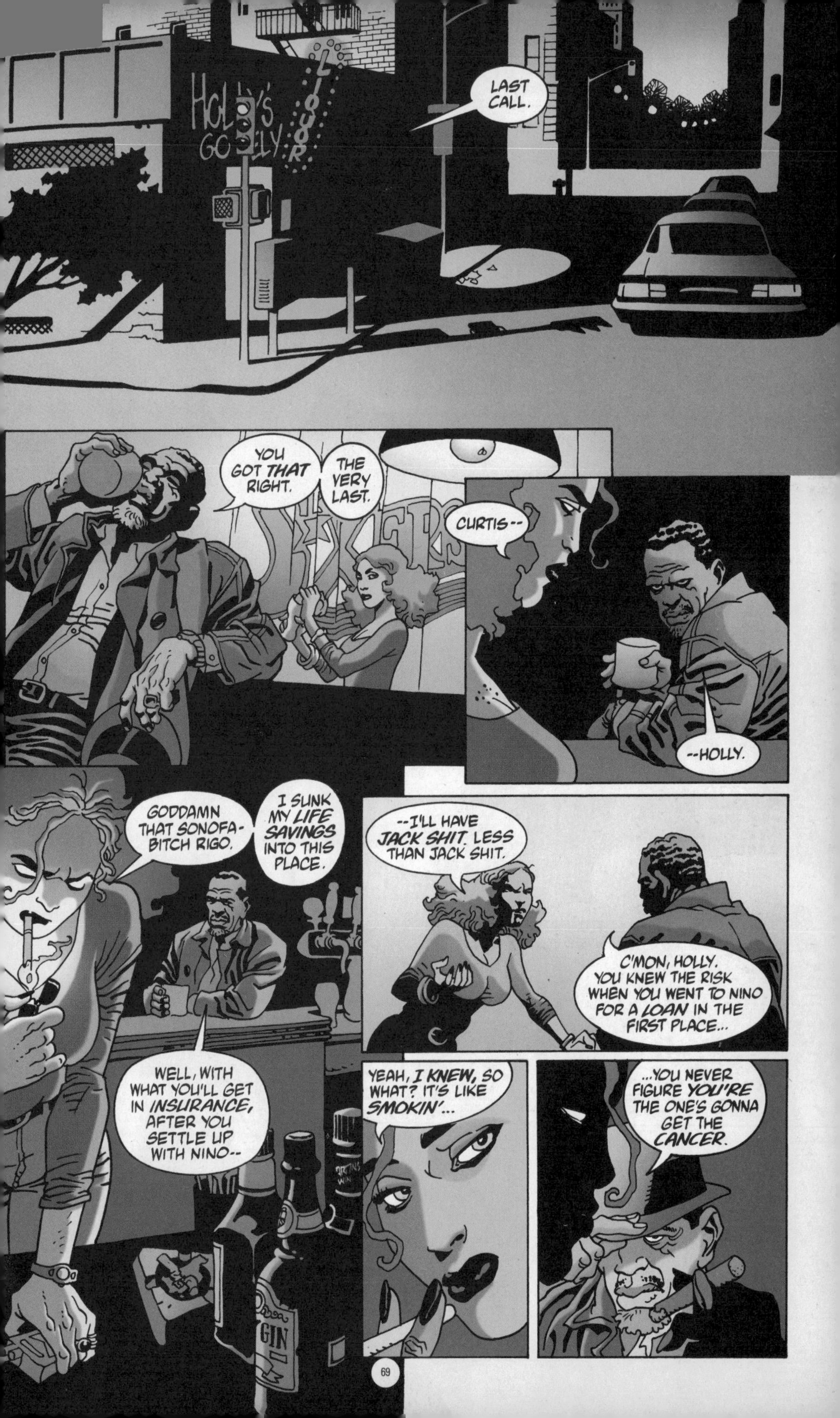
HOLLY'S GOODLY
LIQUOR
LAST CALL.
YOU GOT THAT RIGHT.
THE VERY LAST.
CURTIS--
--HOLLY.
GODDAMN THAT SONOFABITCH RIGO.
I SUNK MY LIFE SAVINGS INTO THIS PLACE.
WELL, WITH WHAT YOU'LL GET IN INSURANCE, AFTER YOU SETTLE UP WITH NINO--
--I'LL HAVE JACK SHIT. LESS THAN JACK SHIT.
C'MON, HOLLY. YOU KNEW THE RISK WHEN YOU WENT TO NINO FOR A LOAN IN THE FIRST PLACE...
YEAH, I KNEW, SO WHAT? IT'S LIKE SMOKIN'...
...YOU NEVER FIGURE YOU'RE THE ONE'S GONNA GET THE CANCER.
GIN

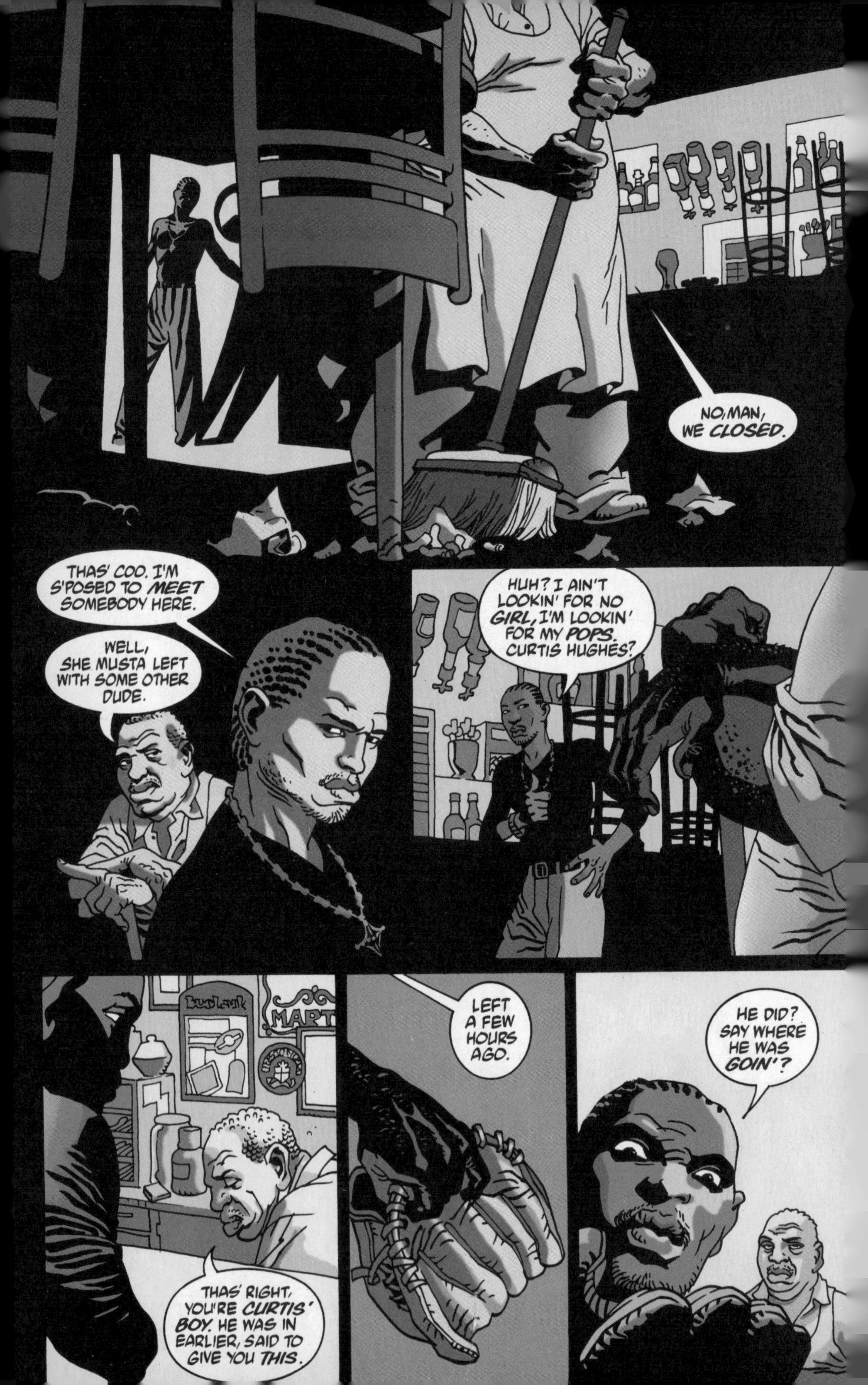
NO, MAN, WE CLOSED.
THAS' COO. I'M S'POSED TO MEET SOMEBODY HERE.
WELL, SHE MUSTA LEFT WITH SOME OTHER DUDE.
HUH? I AIN'T LOOKIN' FOR NO GIRL, I'M LOOKIN' FOR MY POPS. CURTIS HUGHES?
THAS' RIGHT, YOU'RE CURTIS' BOY. HE WAS IN EARLIER, SAID TO GIVE YOU THIS.
LEFT A FEW HOURS AGO.
HE DID? SAY WHERE HE WAS GOIN'?

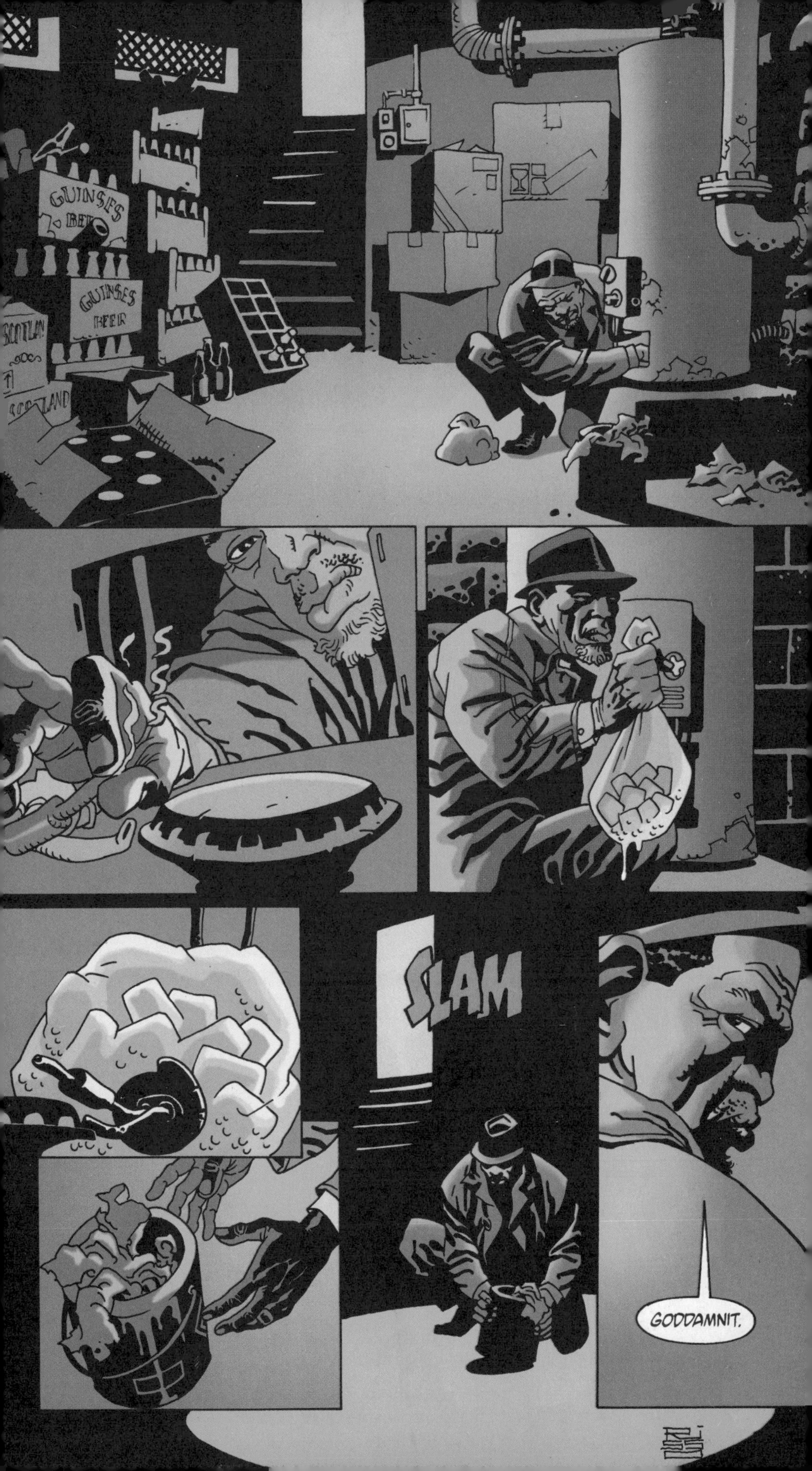

GUINSES BEER
GUINSES BEER
SCOTLAND
SCOTLAND
SLAM
GODDAMNIT.

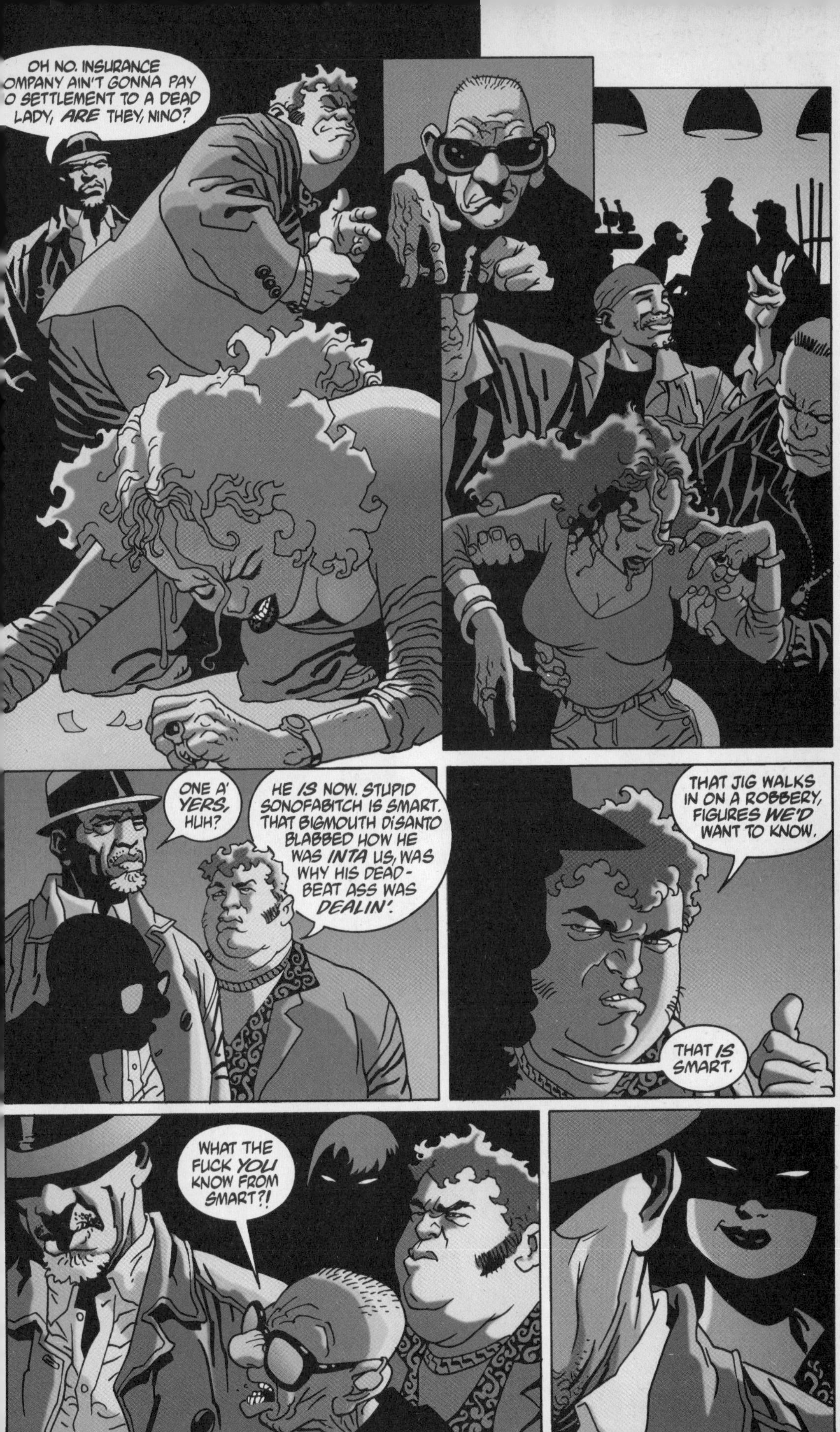
OH NO. INSURANCE
OMPANY AIN'T GONNA PAY
O SETTLEMENT TO A DEAD
LADY, ARE THEY, NINO?
ONE A' YERS, HUH?
HE IS NOW. STUPID SONOFABITCH IS SMART. THAT BIGMOUTH DiSANTO BLABBED HOW HE WAS INTA US, WAS WHY HIS DEAD-BEAT ASS WAS DEALIN'.
THAT JIG WALKS IN ON A ROBBERY, FIGURES WE'D WANT TO KNOW.
THAT IS SMART.
WHAT THE FUCK YOU KNOW FROM SMART?!

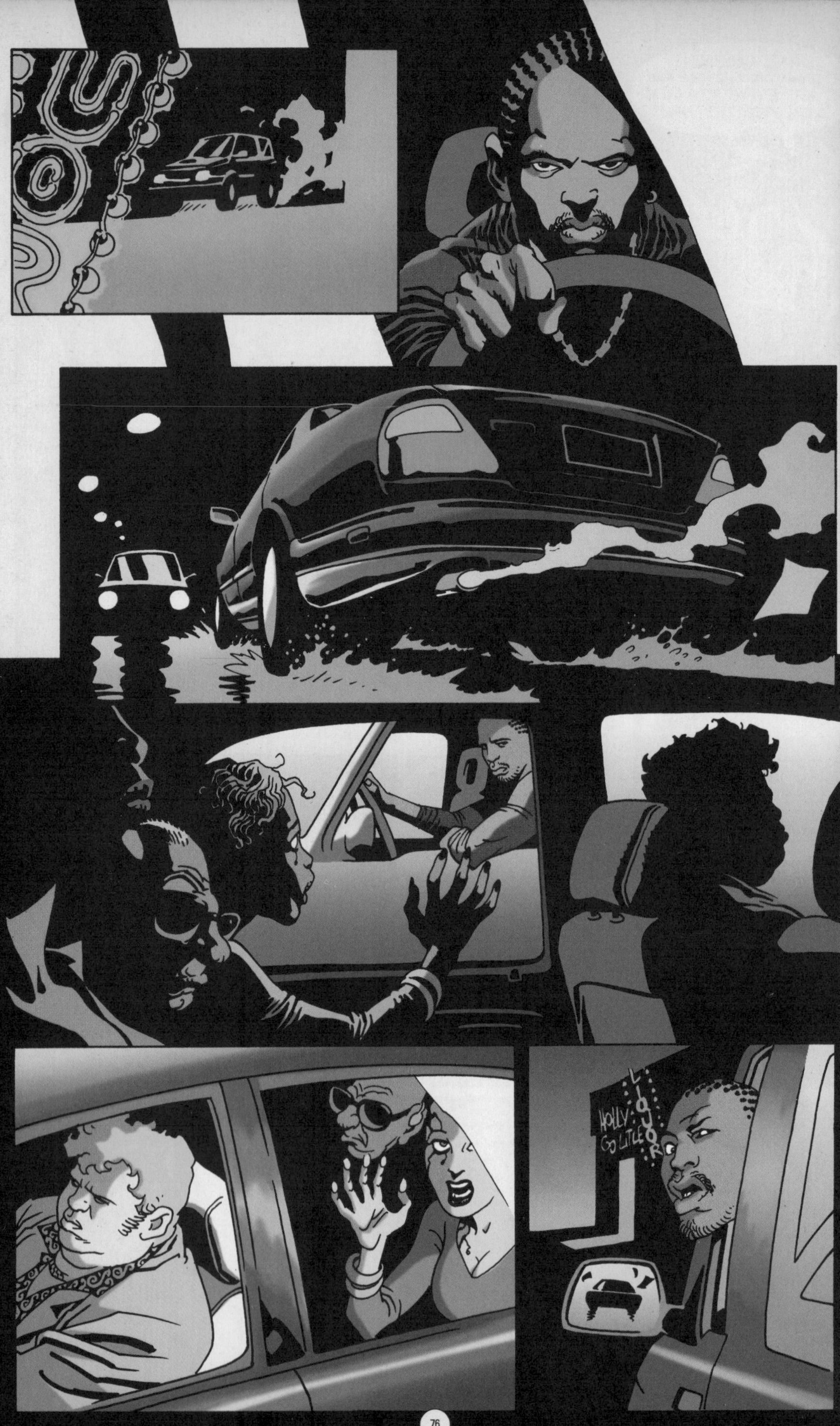
HOLLY GO LITLE
LIQUOR

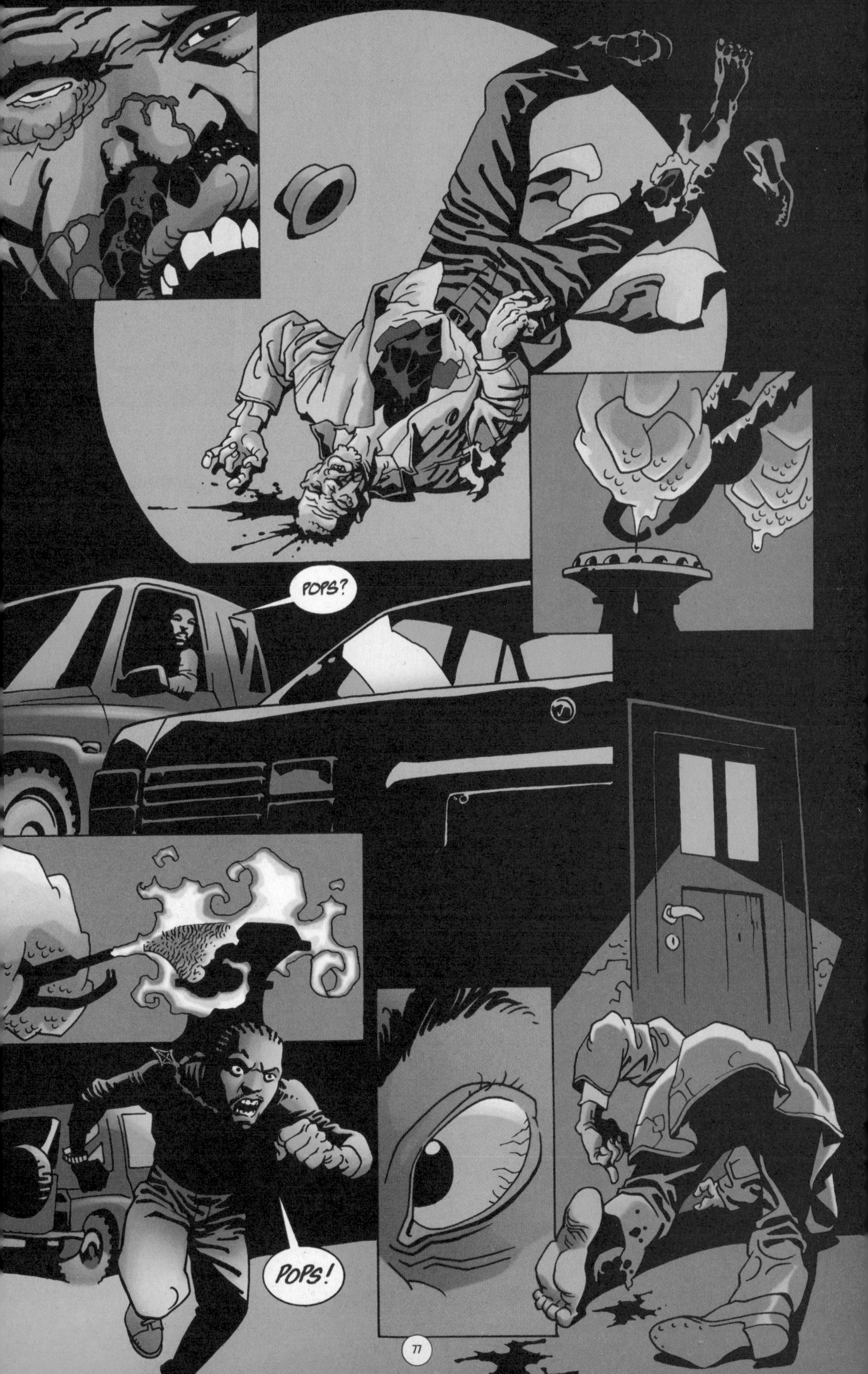
POPS?
POPS!

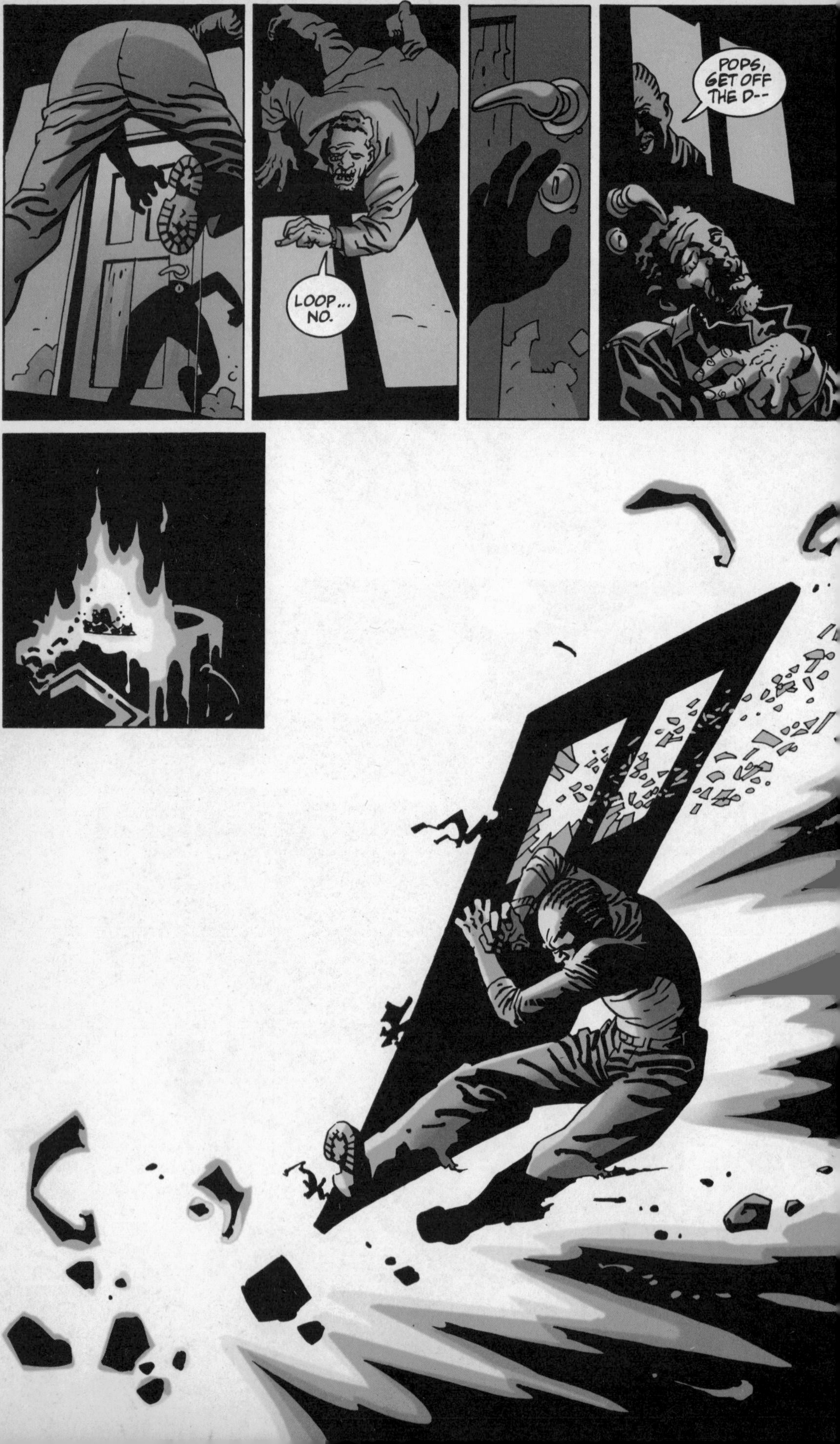
LOOP... NO.
POPS, GET OFF THE D--

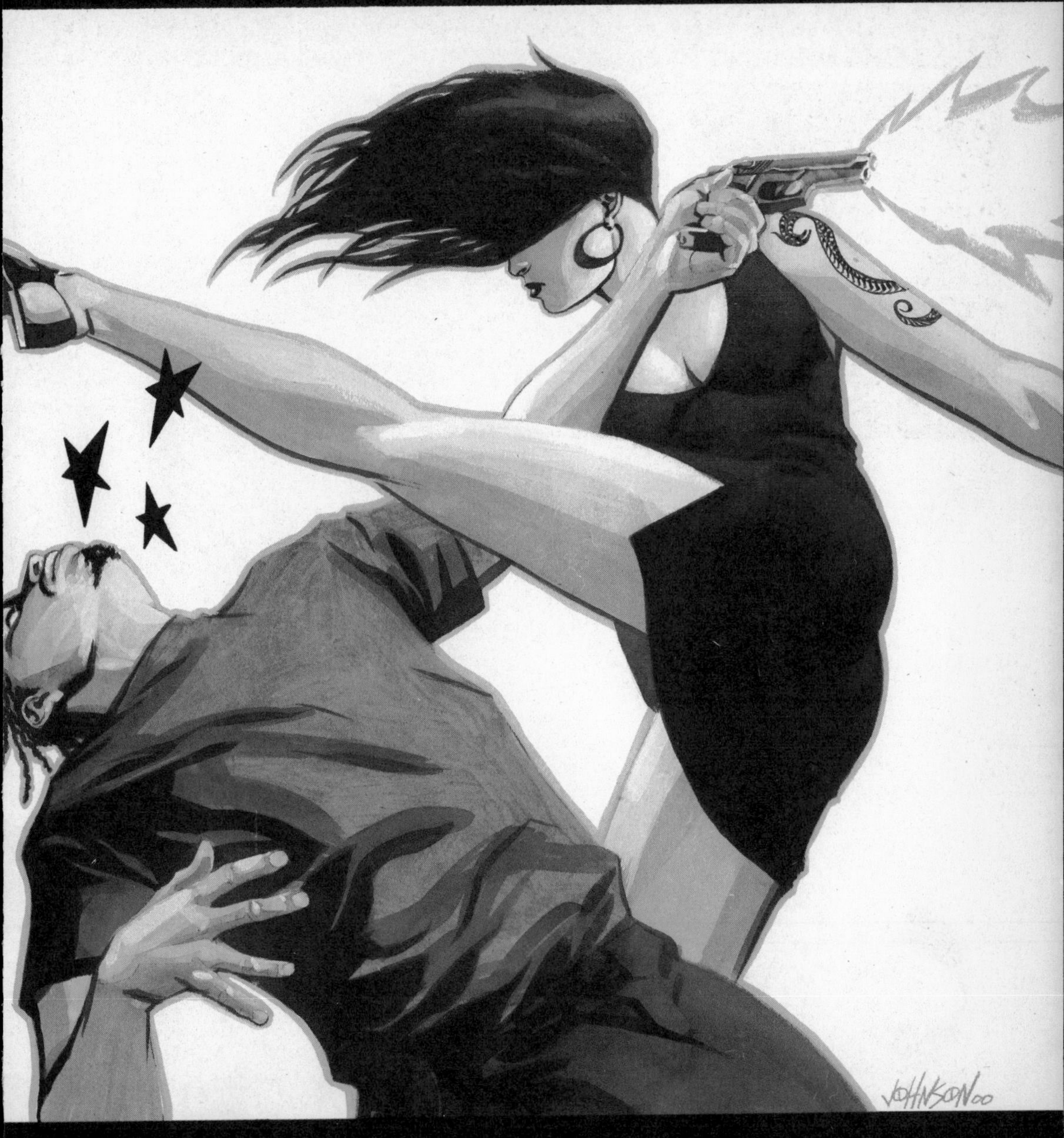
JOHNSON00

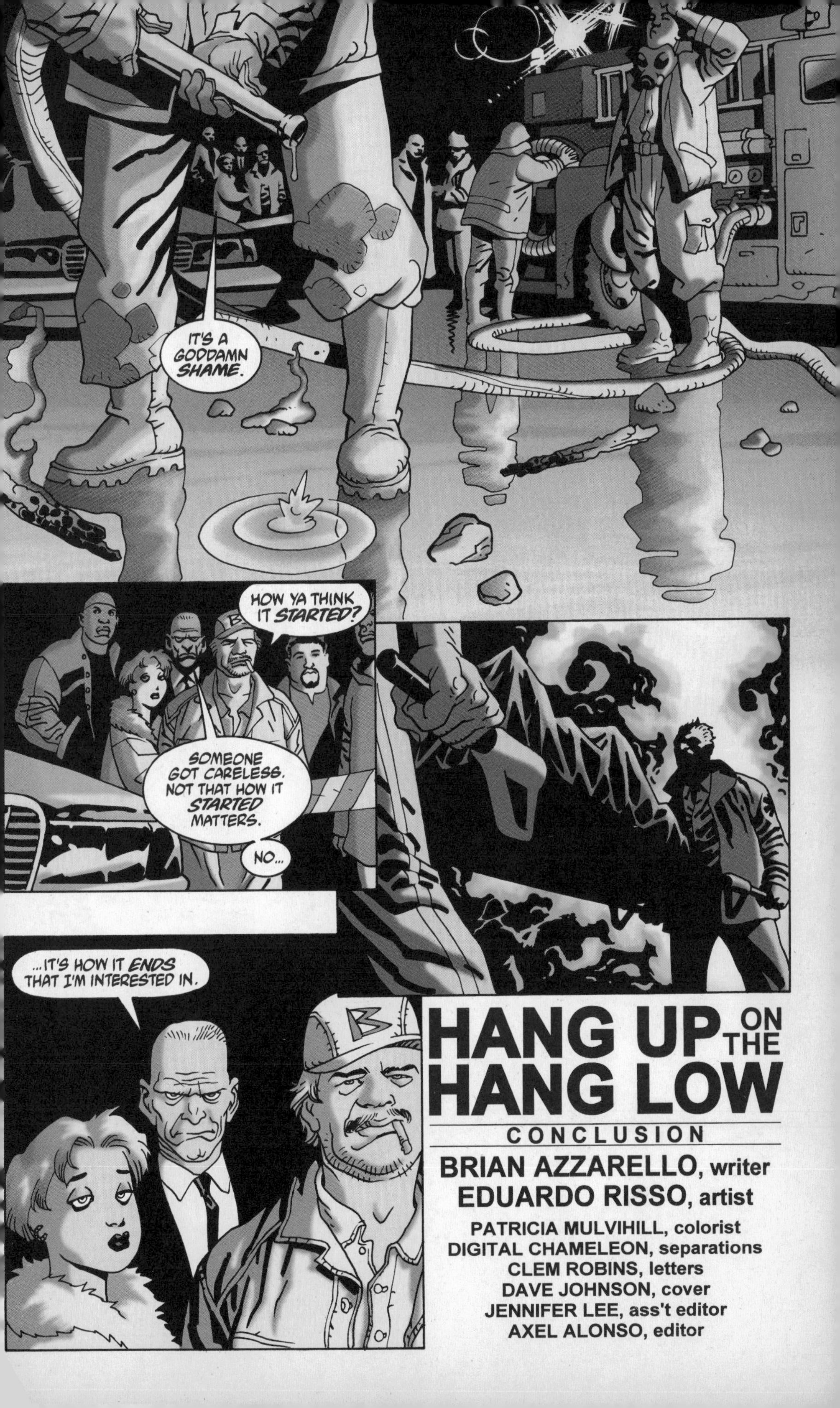

IT'S A GODDAMN SHAME.
HOW YA THINK IT STARTED?
SOMEONE GOT CARELESS. NOT THAT HOW IT STARTED MATTERS.
NO...
...IT'S HOW IT ENDS THAT I'M INTERESTED IN.
HANG UP ON THE HANG LOW
CONCLUSION
BRIAN AZZARELLO, writer
EDUARDO RISSO, artist
PATRICIA MULVIHILL, colorist
DIGITAL CHAMELEON, separations
CLEM ROBINS, letters
DAVE JOHNSON, cover
JENNIFER LEE, ass't editor
AXEL ALONSO, editor

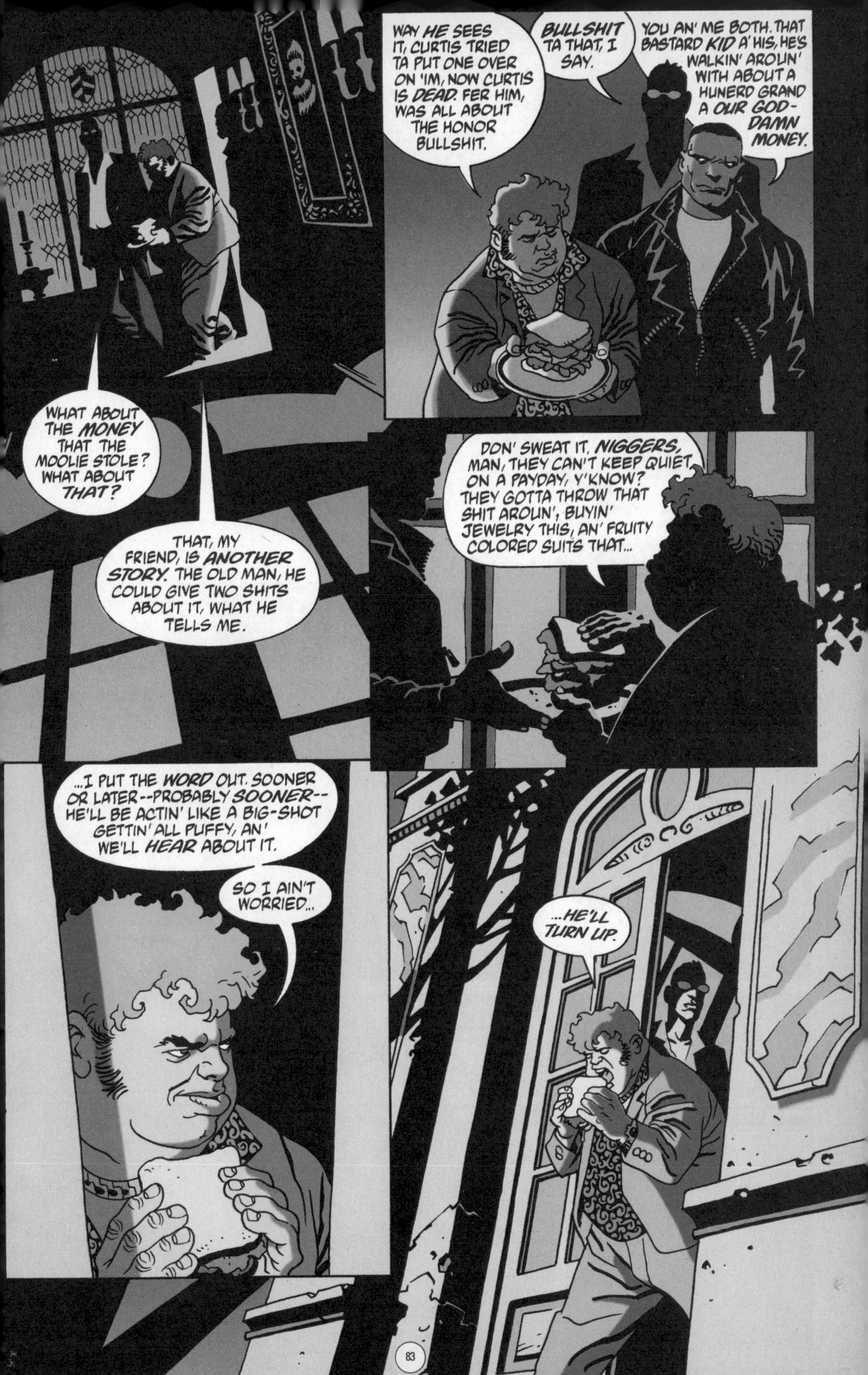
WAY HE SEES IT, CURTIS TRIED TA PUT ONE OVER ON 'IM, NOW CURTIS IS DEAD. FER HIM, WAS ALL ABOUT THE HONOR BULLSHIT.
BULLSHIT TA THAT, I SAY.
YOU AN' ME BOTH. THAT BASTARD KID A' HIS, HE'S WALKIN' AROUN' WITH ABOUT A HUNERD GRAND A OUR GOD-DAMN MONEY.
WHAT ABOUT THE MONEY THAT THE MOOLIE STOLE? WHAT ABOUT THAT?
THAT, MY FRIEND, IS ANOTHER STORY. THE OLD MAN, HE COULD GIVE TWO SHITS ABOUT IT, WHAT HE TELLS ME.
DON' SWEAT IT, NIGGERS, MAN, THEY CAN'T KEEP QUIET ON A PAYDAY, Y'KNOW? THEY GOTTA THROW THAT SHIT AROUN', BUYIN' JEWELRY THIS, AN' FRUITY COLORED SUITS THAT...
...I PUT THE WORD OUT. SOONER OR LATER--PROBABLY SOONER--HE'LL BE ACTIN' LIKE A BIG-SHOT GETTIN' ALL PUFFY, AN' WE'LL HEAR ABOUT IT.
SO I AIN'T WORRIED...
...HE'LL TURN UP.

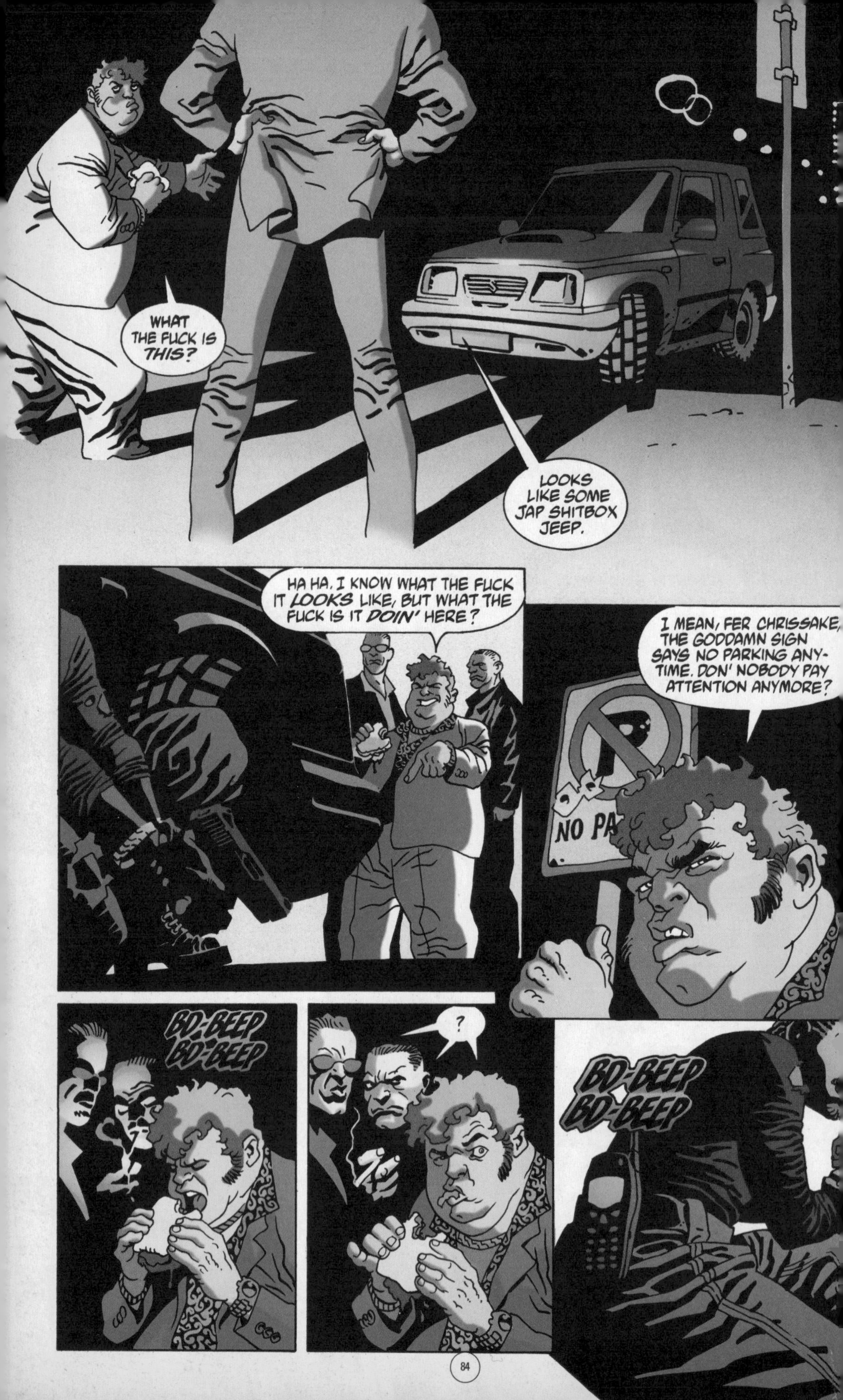

WHAT THE FUCK IS THIS?
LOOKS LIKE SOME JAP SHITBOX JEEP.
HA HA. I KNOW WHAT THE FUCK IT LOOKS LIKE, BUT WHAT THE FUCK IS IT DOIN' HERE?
I MEAN, FER CHRISSAKE, THE GODDAMN SIGN SAYS NO PARKING ANY-TIME. DON' NOBODY PAY ATTENTION ANYMORE?
NO PA
BD-BEEP BD-BEEP
?
BD-BEEP BD-BEEP

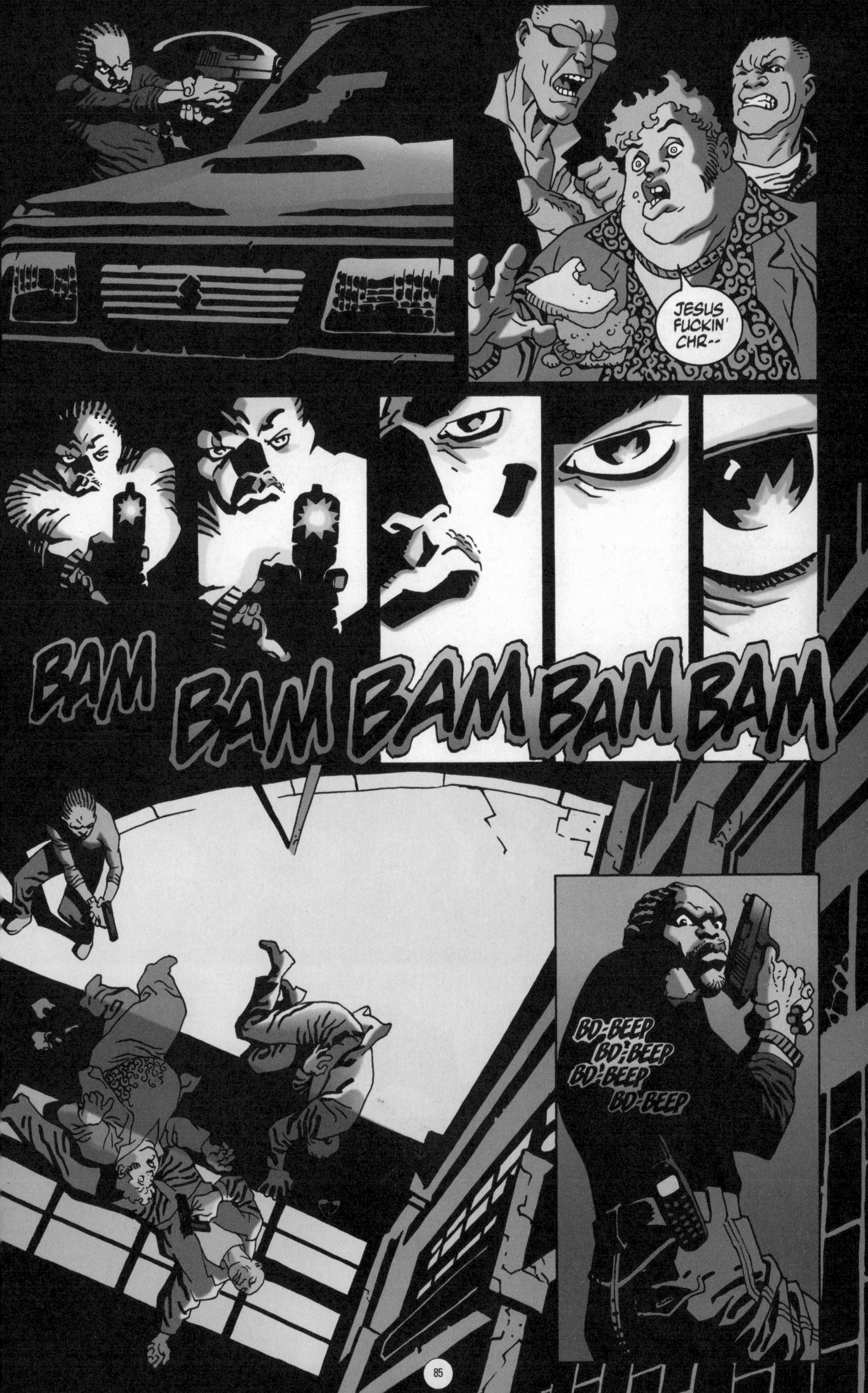
JESUS FUCKIN' CHR--
BAM
BAM BAM BAM BAM
BD-BEEP
BD-BEEP
BD-BEEP
BD-BEEP

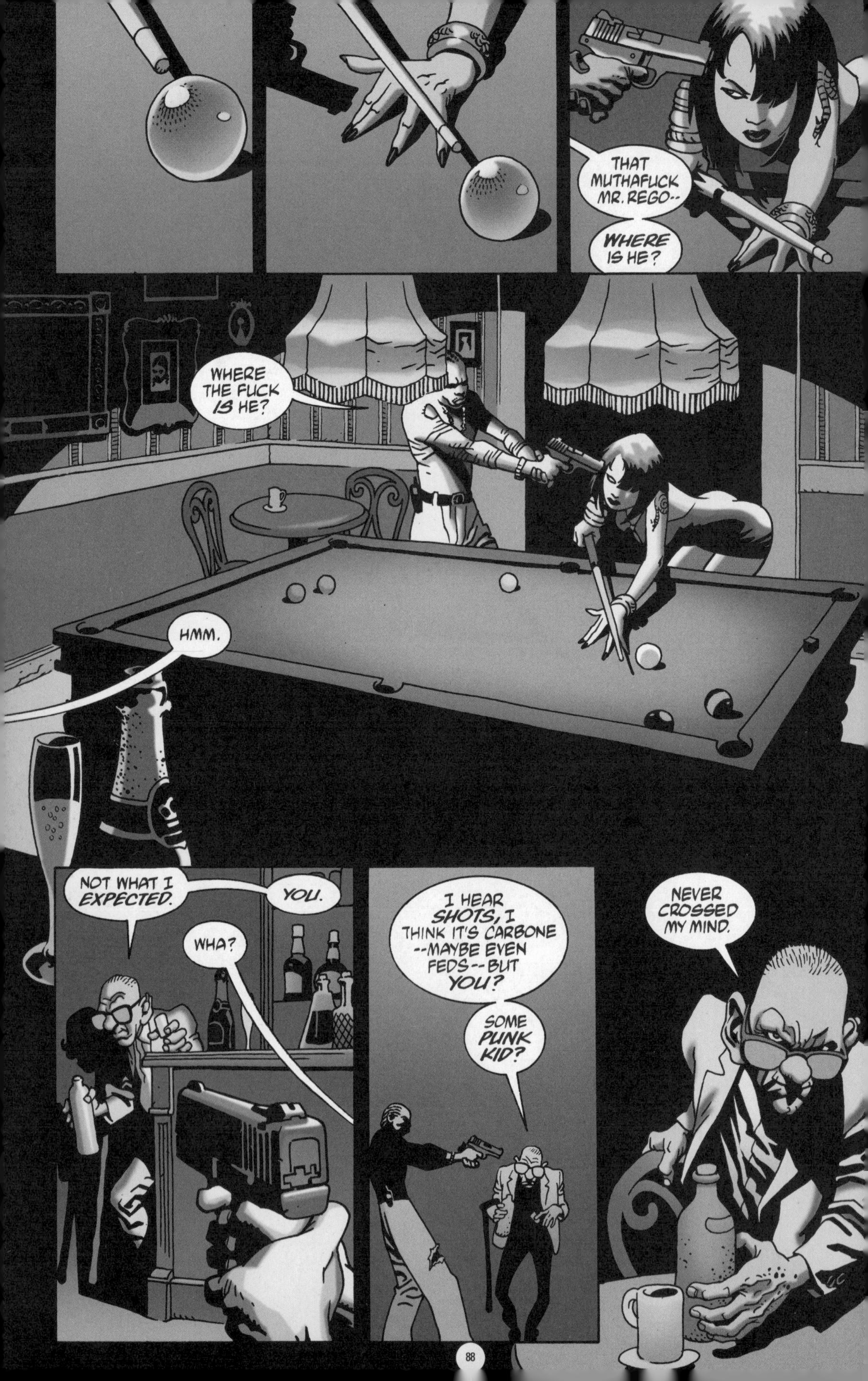

THAT MUTHAFUCK MR. REGO--
WHERE IS HE?
WHERE THE FUCK IS HE?
HMM.
NOT WHAT I EXPECTED.
YOU.
WHA?
I HEAR SHOTS, I THINK IT'S CARBONE --MAYBE EVEN FEDS--BUT YOU?
SOME PUNK KID?
NEVER CROSSED MY MIND.

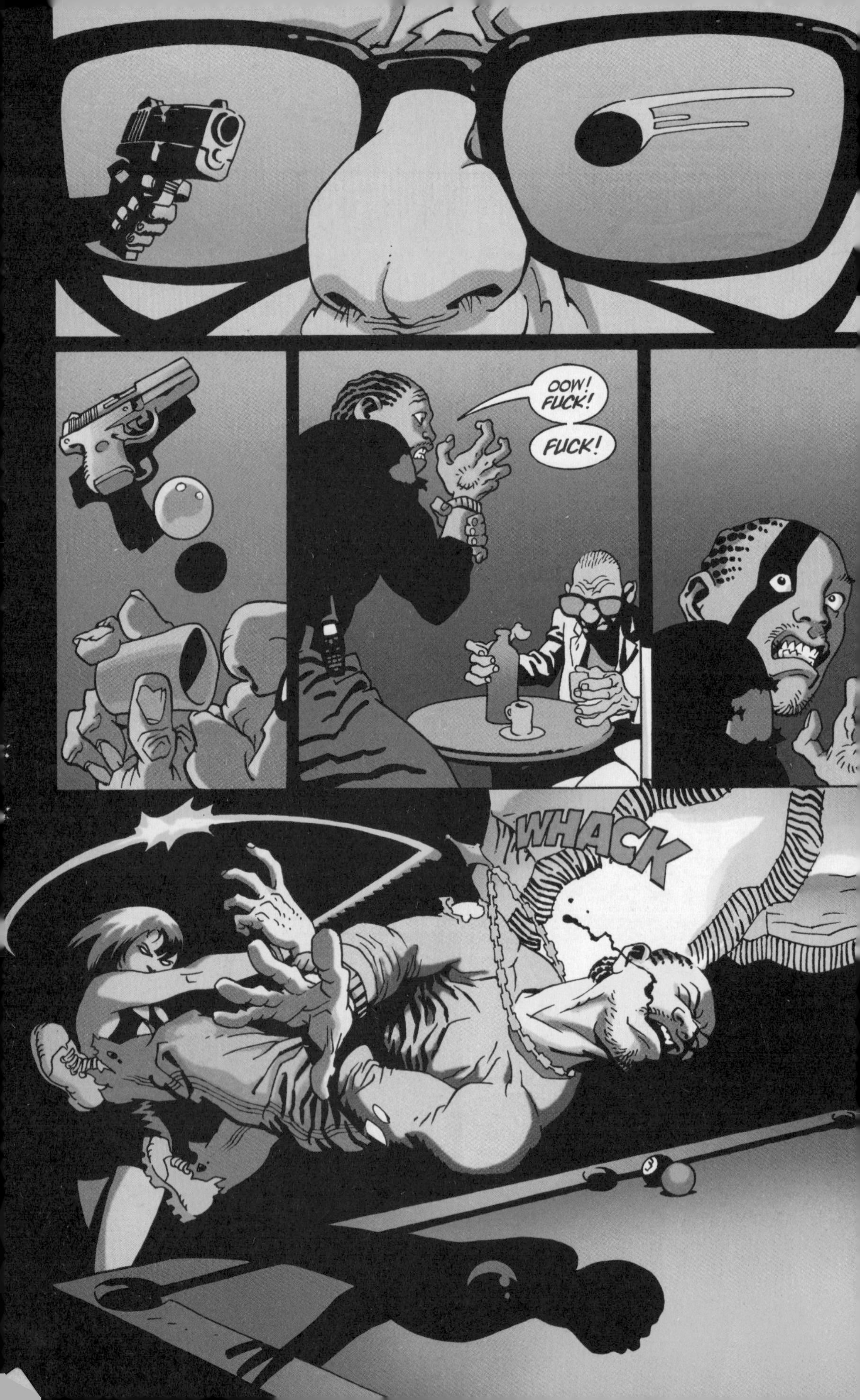
OOW! FUCK!
FUCK!
WHACK

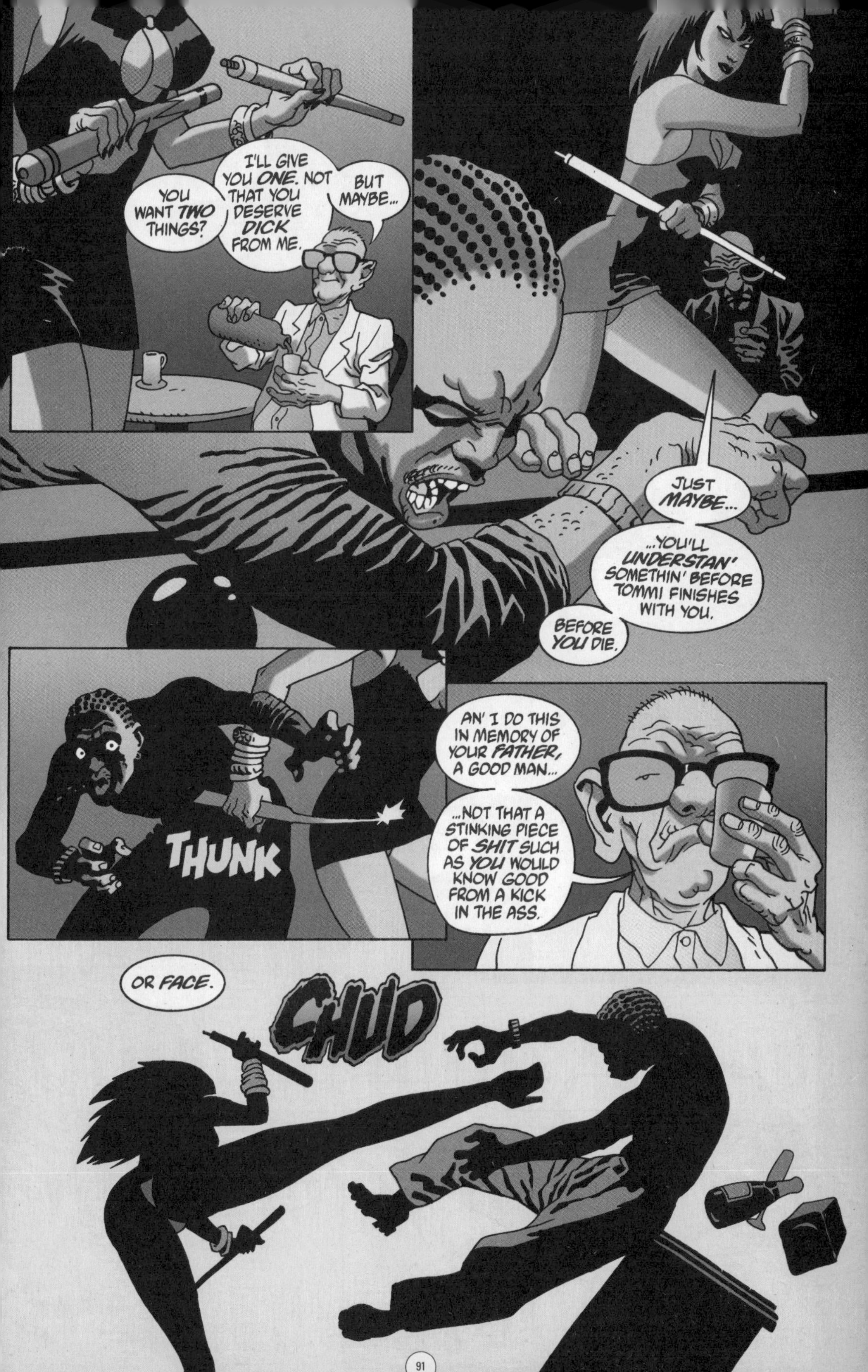
YOU WANT TWO THINGS?
I'LL GIVE YOU ONE. NOT THAT YOU DESERVE DICK FROM ME.
BUT MAYBE...
JUST MAYBE...
...YOU'LL UNDERSTAN' SOMETHIN' BEFORE TOMMI FINISHES WITH YOU.
BEFORE YOU DIE.
THUNK
AN' I DO THIS IN MEMORY OF YOUR FATHER, A GOOD MAN...
...NOT THAT A STINKING PIECE OF SHIT SUCH AS YOU WOULD KNOW GOOD FROM A KICK IN THE ASS.
OR FACE.
CHUD

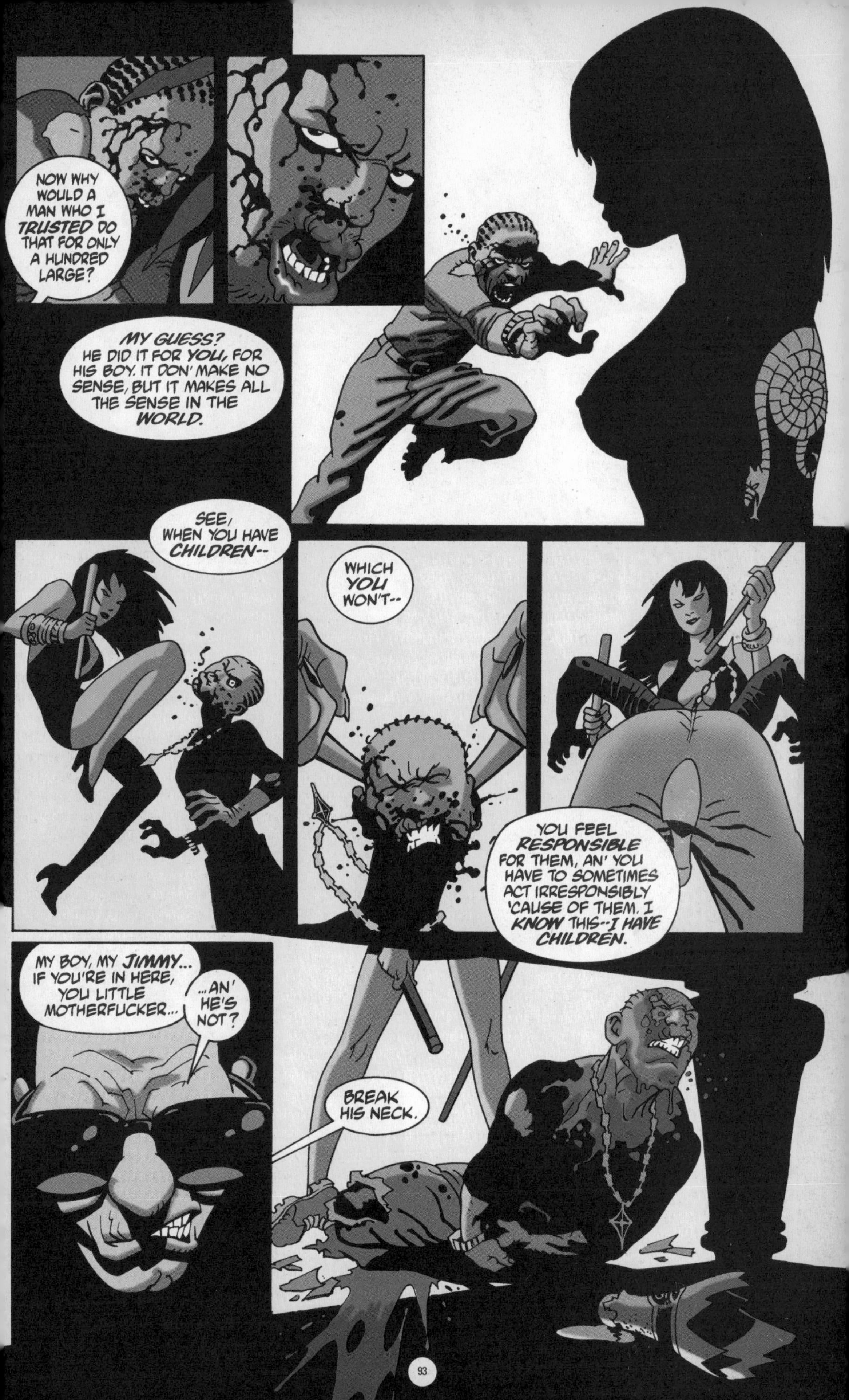
NOW WHY WOULD A MAN WHO I TRUSTED DO THAT FOR ONLY A HUNDRED LARGE?
MY GUESS? HE DID IT FOR YOU, FOR HIS BOY. IT DON' MAKE NO SENSE, BUT IT MAKES ALL THE SENSE IN THE WORLD.
SEE, WHEN YOU HAVE CHILDREN--
WHICH YOU WON'T--
YOU FEEL RESPONSIBLE FOR THEM, AN' YOU HAVE TO SOMETIMES ACT IRRESPONSIBLY 'CAUSE OF THEM. I KNOW THIS--I HAVE CHILDREN.
MY BOY, MY JIMMY... IF YOU'RE IN HERE, YOU LITTLE MOTHERFUCKER...
...AN' HE'S NOT?
BREAK HIS NECK.

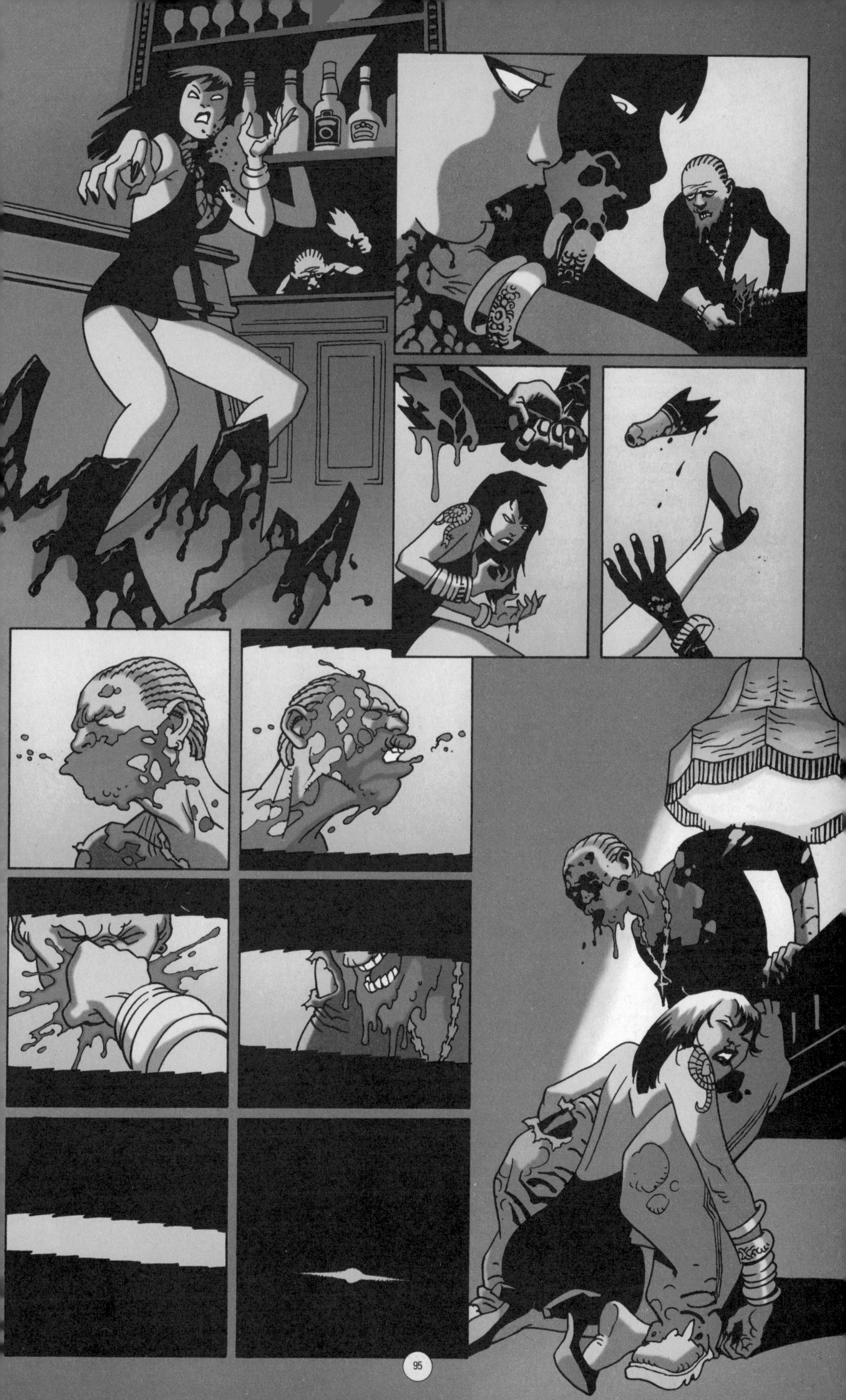

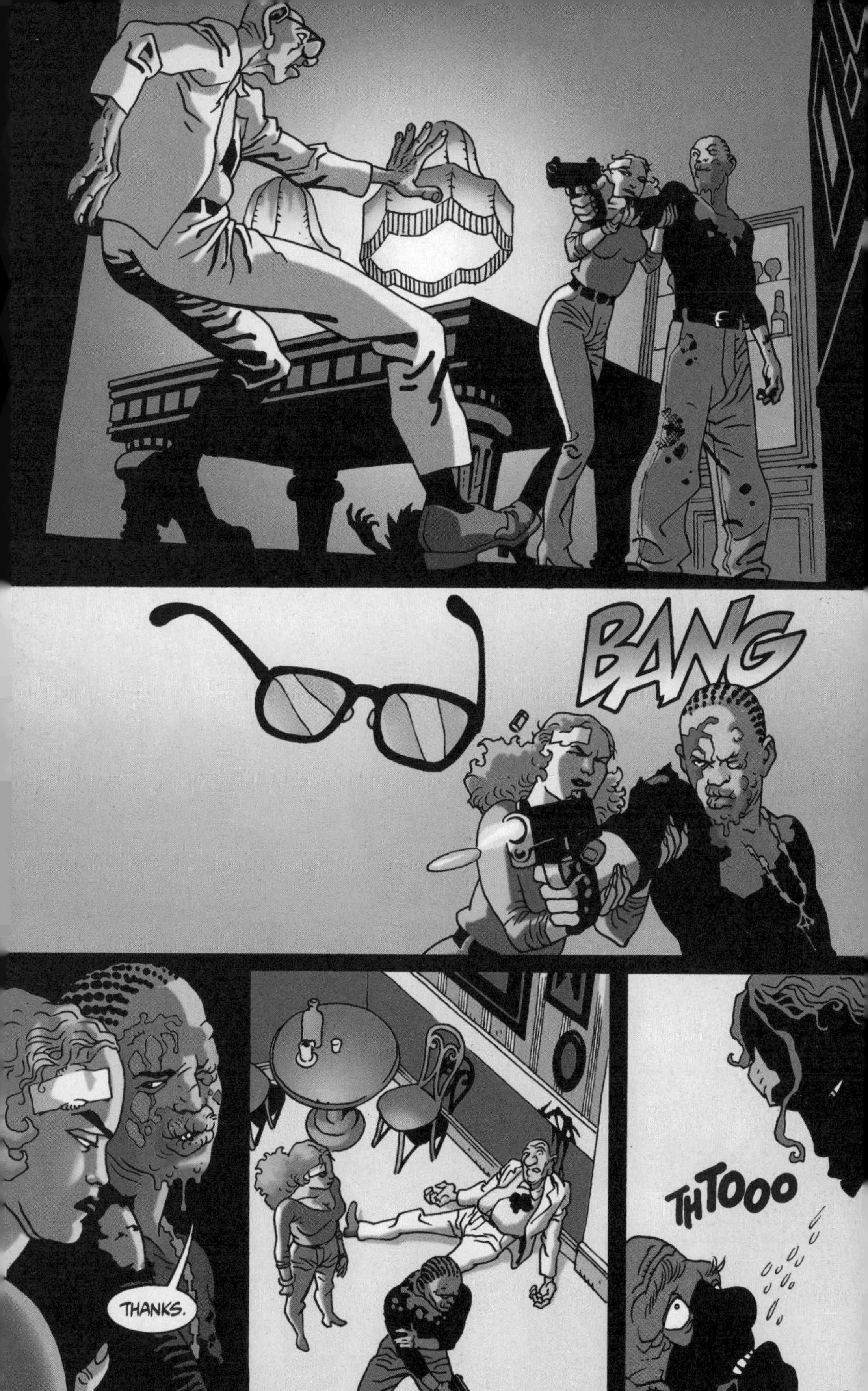
BANG
THANKS.
THTOOO

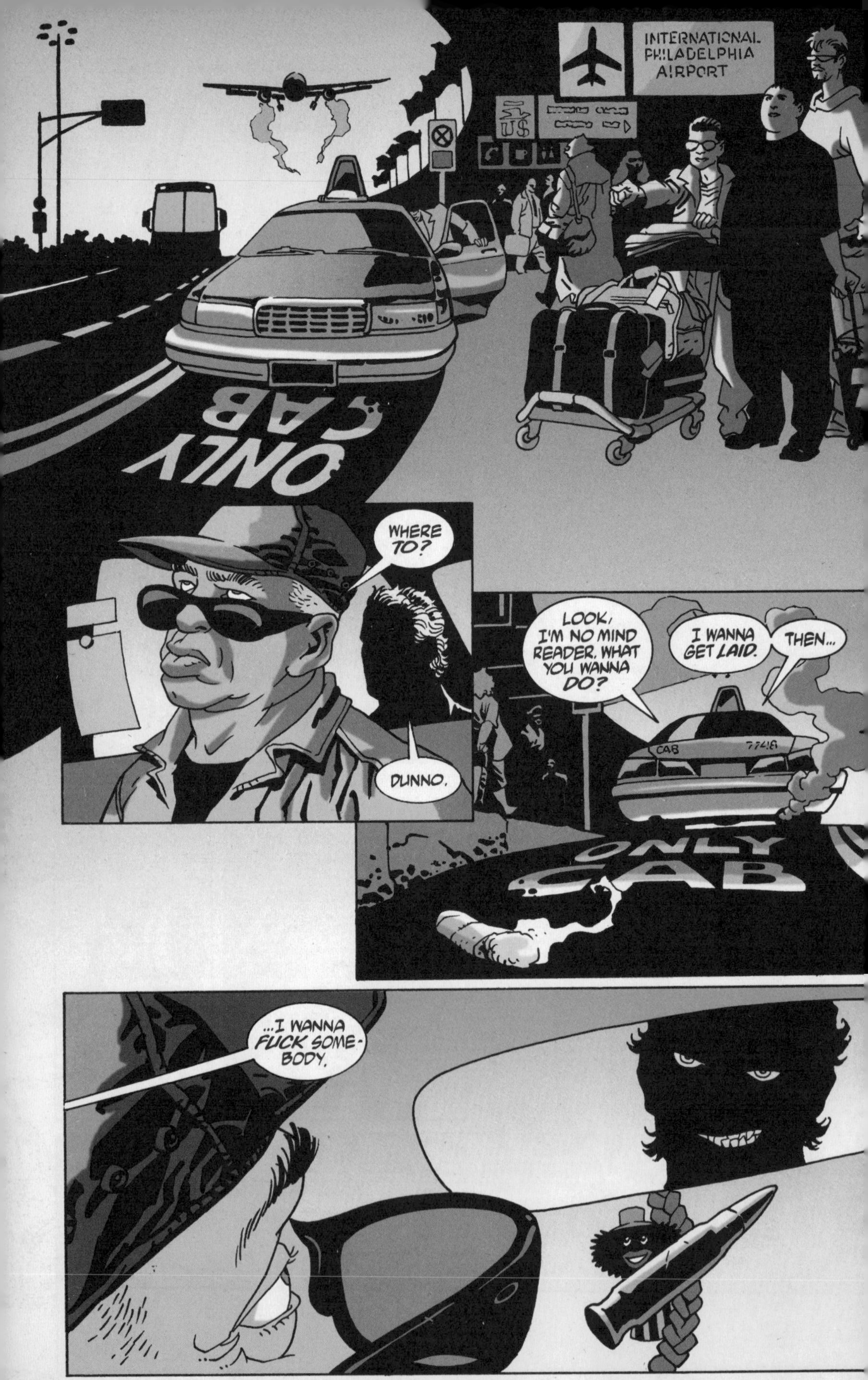
INTERNATIONAL PHILADELPHIA AIRPORT
ONLY CAB
WHERE TO?
DUNNO.
LOOK, I'M NO MIND READER. WHAT YOU WANNA DO?
I WANNA GET LAID.
THEN...
ONLY CAB
...I WANNA FUCK SOME-BODY.

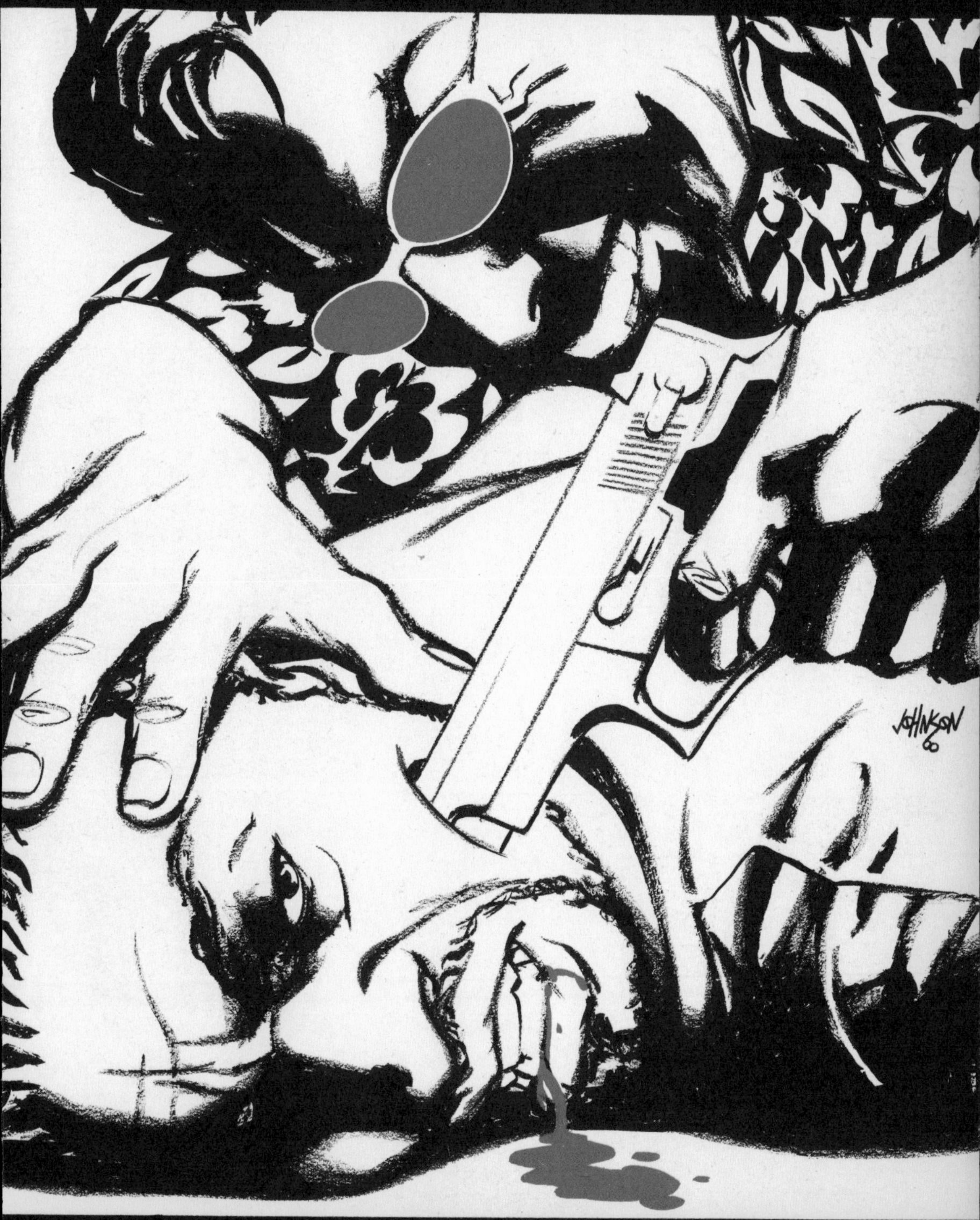
JOHNSON

EPILOGUE FOR A ROAD DOG

BRIAN AZZARELLO WRITER

EDUARDO RISSO ARTIST

PATRICIA MULVIHILL COLORIST

DIGITAL CHAMELEON SEPARATIONS

CLEM ROBINS LETTERS

DAVE JOHNSON COVER

JENNIFER LEE ASST. EDITOR

AXEL ALONSO EDITOR

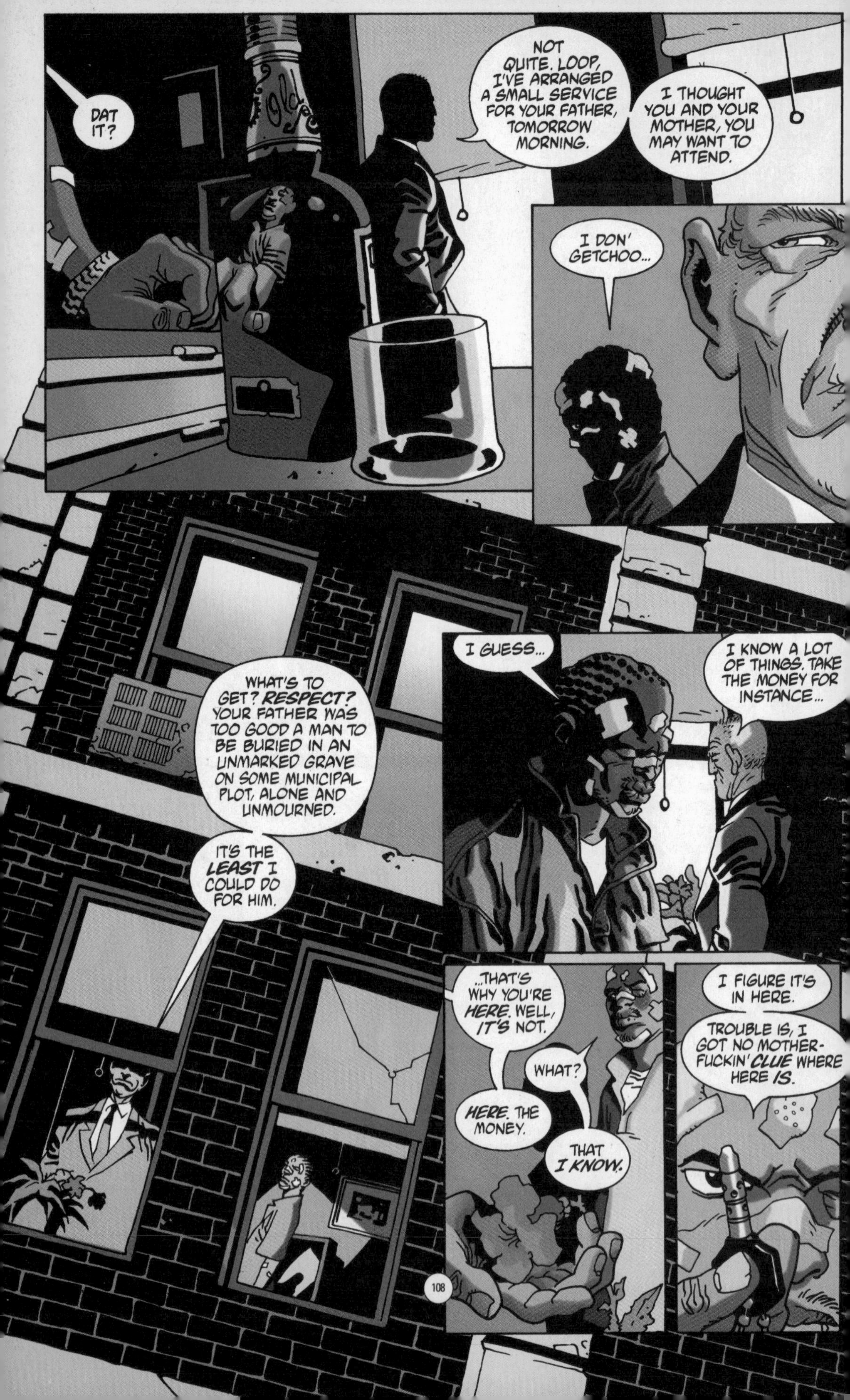
DAT IT?
NOT QUITE. LOOP, I'VE ARRANGED A SMALL SERVICE FOR YOUR FATHER, TOMORROW MORNING.
I THOUGHT YOU AND YOUR MOTHER, YOU MAY WANT TO ATTEND.
I DON' GETCHOO...
WHAT'S TO GET? RESPECT? YOUR FATHER WAS TOO GOOD A MAN TO BE BURIED IN AN UNMARKED GRAVE ON SOME MUNICIPAL PLOT, ALONE AND UNMOURNED.
IT'S THE LEAST I COULD DO FOR HIM.
I GUESS...
I KNOW A LOT OF THINGS. TAKE THE MONEY FOR INSTANCE...
...THAT'S WHY YOU'RE HERE. WELL, IT'S NOT.
WHAT?
HERE. THE MONEY.
THAT I KNOW.
I FIGURE IT'S IN HERE.
TROUBLE IS, I GOT NO MOTHER-FUCKIN' CLUE WHERE HERE IS.

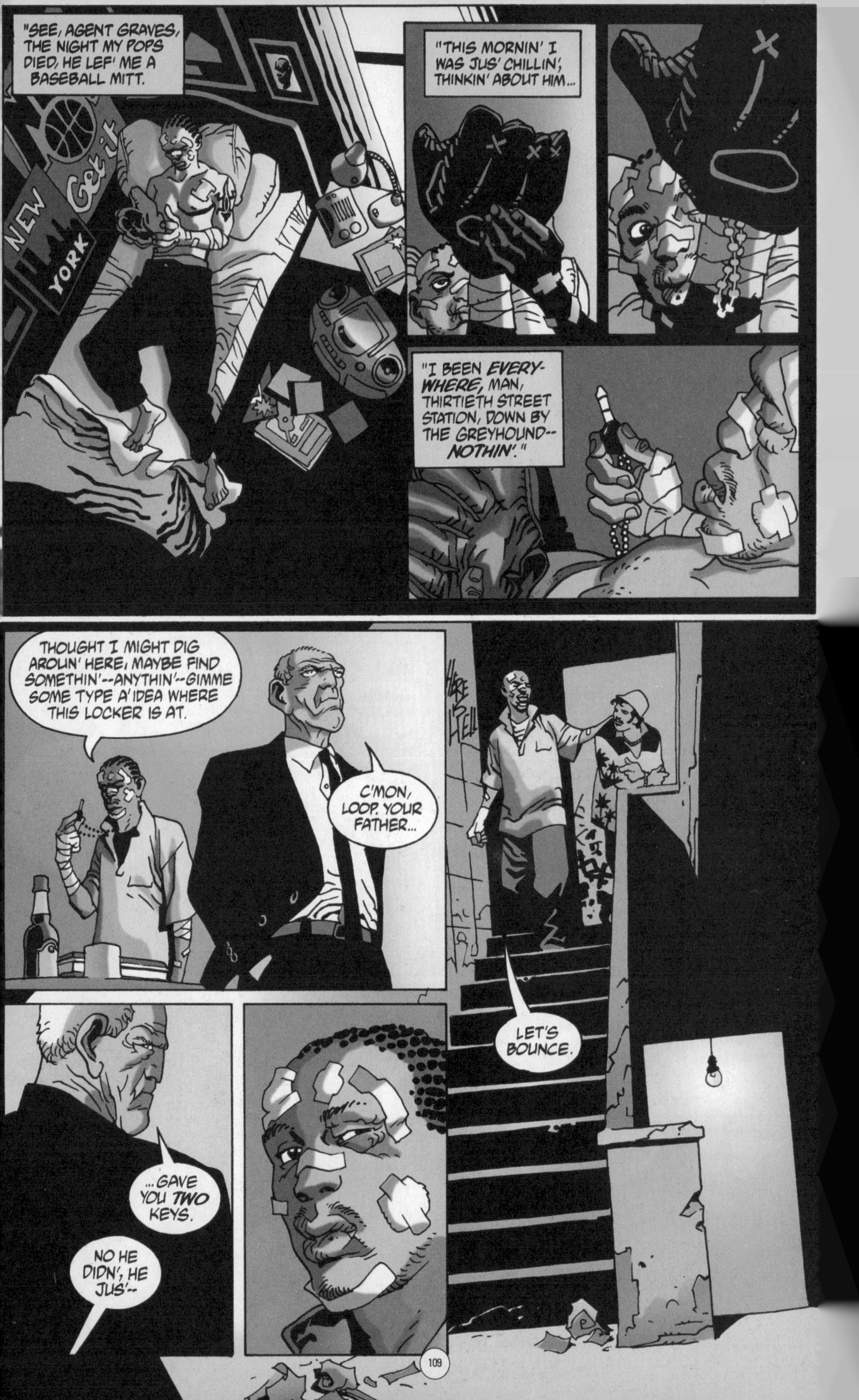

"SEE, AGENT GRAVES, THE NIGHT MY POPS DIED, HE LEF' ME A BASEBALL MITT.
NEW YORK
Get it
"THIS MORNIN' I WAS JUS' CHILLIN', THINKIN' ABOUT HIM...
"I BEEN EVERY-WHERE, MAN, THIRTIETH STREET STATION, DOWN BY THE GREYHOUND-- NOTHIN'."
THOUGHT I MIGHT DIG AROUN' HERE, MAYBE FIND SOMETHIN'--ANYTHIN'--GIMME SOME TYPE A' IDEA WHERE THIS LOCKER IS AT.
C'MON, LOOP. YOUR FATHER...
...GAVE YOU TWO KEYS.
NO HE DIDN', HE JUS'--
LET'S BOUNCE.

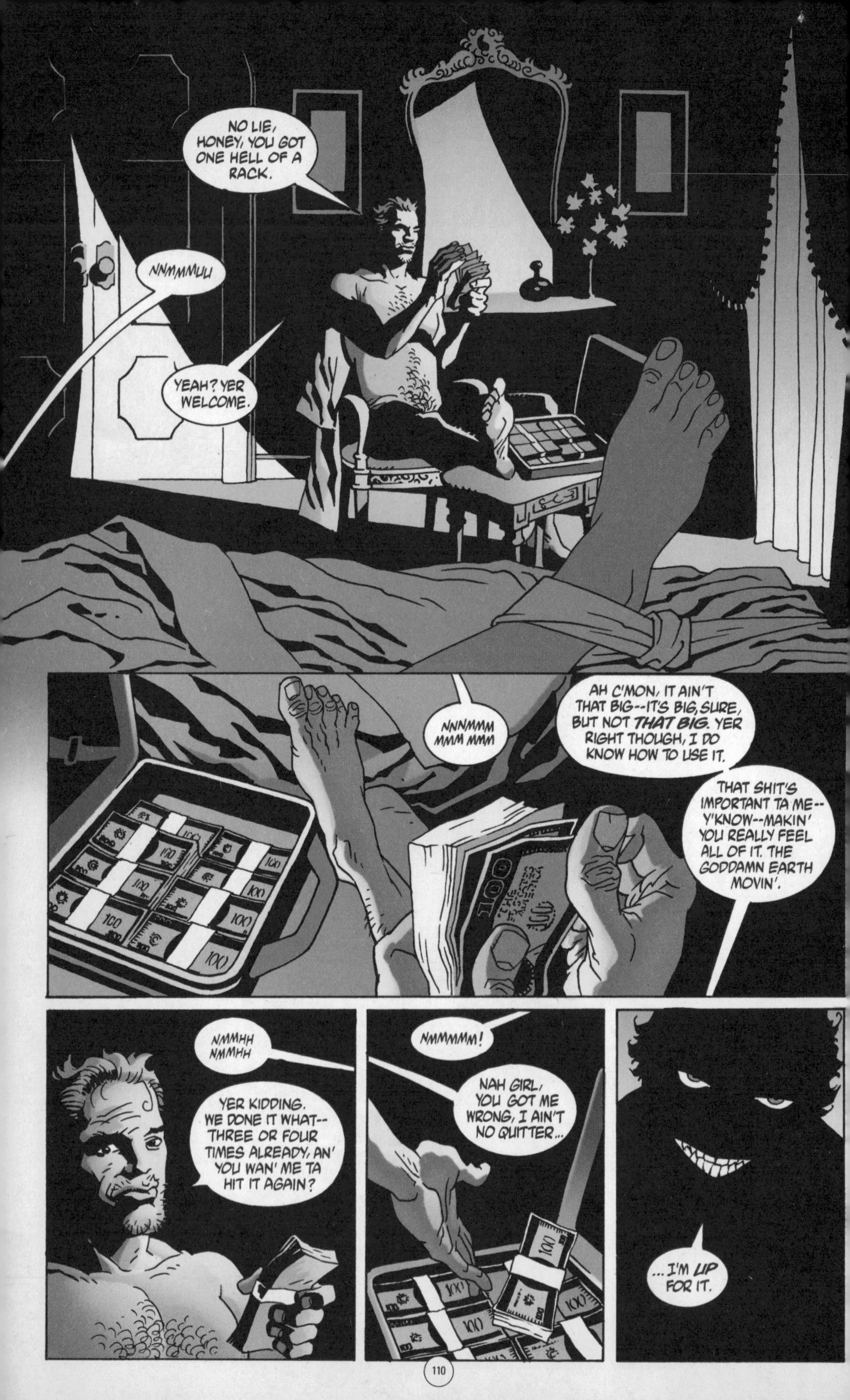

NO LIE, HONEY, YOU GOT ONE HELL OF A RACK.
NNMMMUU
YEAH? YER WELCOME.
NNNMMM MMM MMM
AH C'MON, IT AIN'T THAT BIG--IT'S BIG, SURE, BUT NOT *THAT BIG*. YER RIGHT THOUGH, I DO KNOW HOW TO USE IT.
THAT SHIT'S IMPORTANT TA ME--Y'KNOW--MAKIN' YOU REALLY FEEL ALL OF IT. THE GODDAMN EARTH MOVIN'.
NMMHH NMMHH
YER KIDDING. WE DONE IT WHAT--THREE OR FOUR TIMES ALREADY, AN' YOU WAN' ME TA HIT IT AGAIN?
NMMMMM!
NAH GIRL, YOU GOT ME WRONG, I AIN'T NO QUITTER...
...I'M *UP* FOR IT.

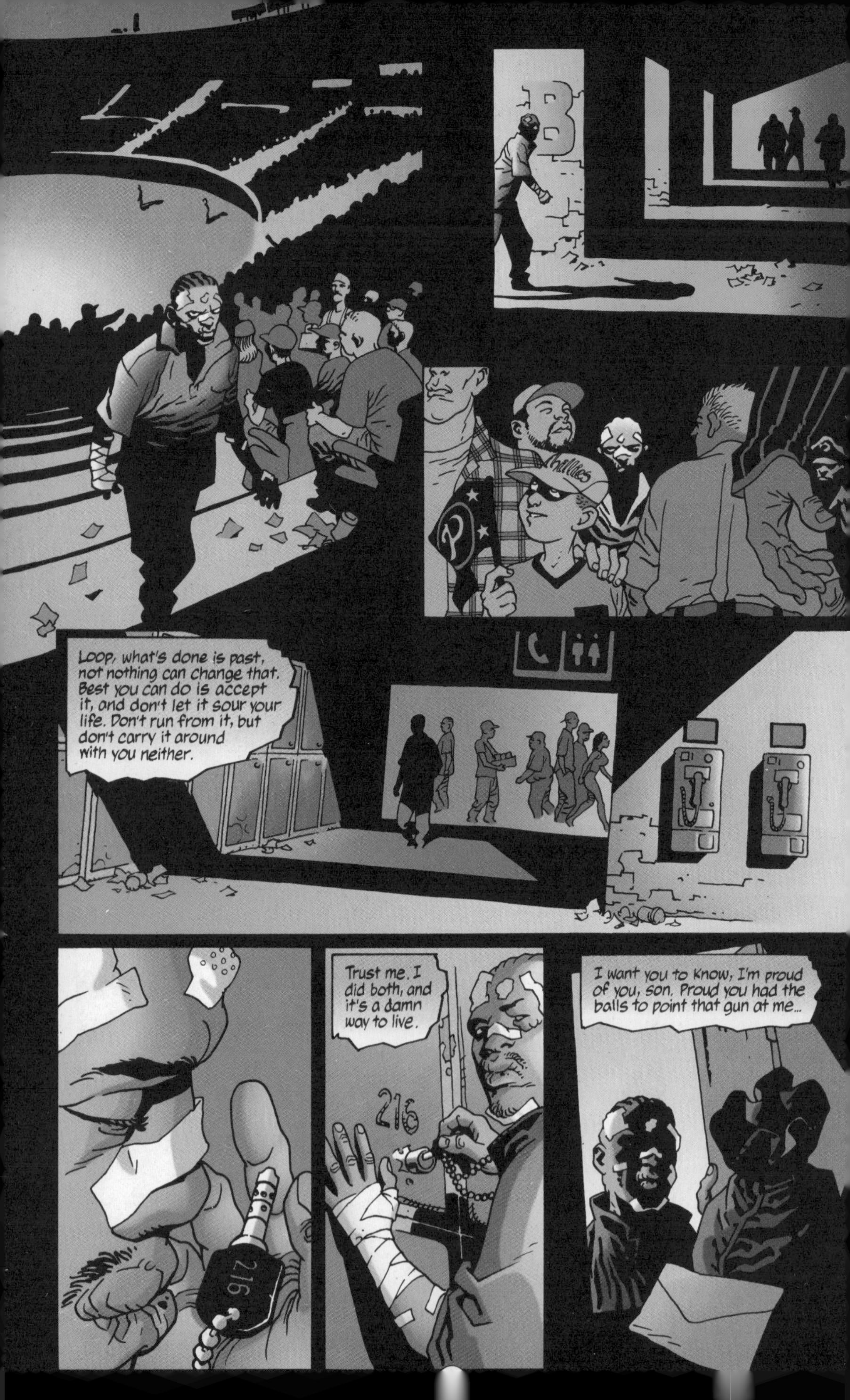
B
Phillies
Loop, what's done is past, not nothing can change that. Best you can do is accept it, and don't let it sour your life. Don't run from it, but don't carry it around with you neither.
Trust me. I did both, and it's a damn way to live.
216
I want you to know, I'm proud of you, son. Proud you had the balls to point that gun at me...

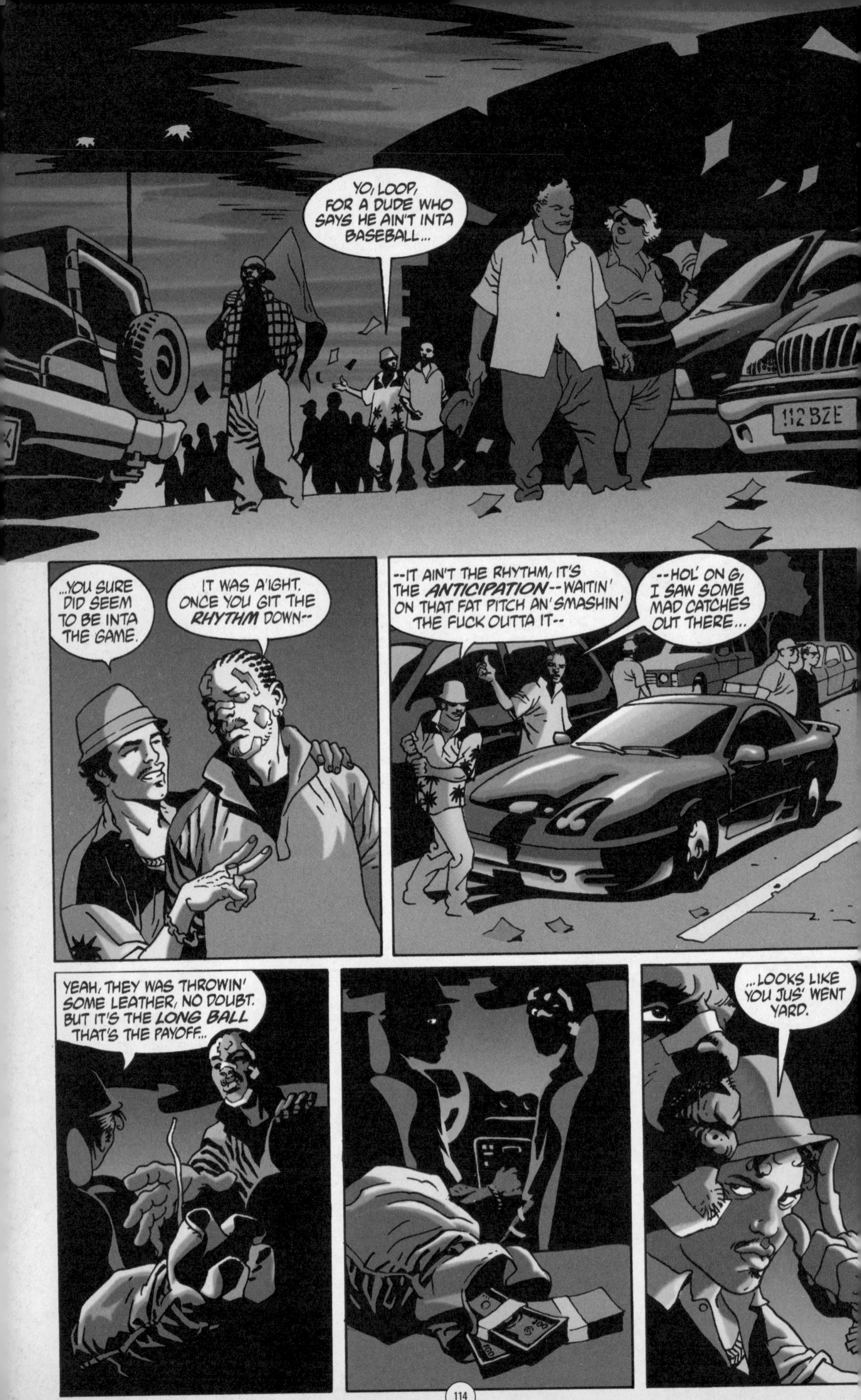
YO, LOOP, FOR A DUDE WHO SAYS HE AIN'T INTA BASEBALL...
112 BZE
...YOU SURE DID SEEM TO BE INTA THE GAME.
IT WAS A'IGHT. ONCE YOU GIT THE RHYTHM DOWN--
--IT AIN'T THE RHYTHM, IT'S THE ANTICIPATION--WAITIN' ON THAT FAT PITCH AN' SMASHIN' THE FUCK OUTTA IT--
--HOL' ON G, I SAW SOME MAD CATCHES OUT THERE...
YEAH, THEY WAS THROWIN' SOME LEATHER, NO DOUBT. BUT IT'S THE LONG BALL THAT'S THE PAYOFF...
...LOOKS LIKE YOU JUS' WENT YARD.

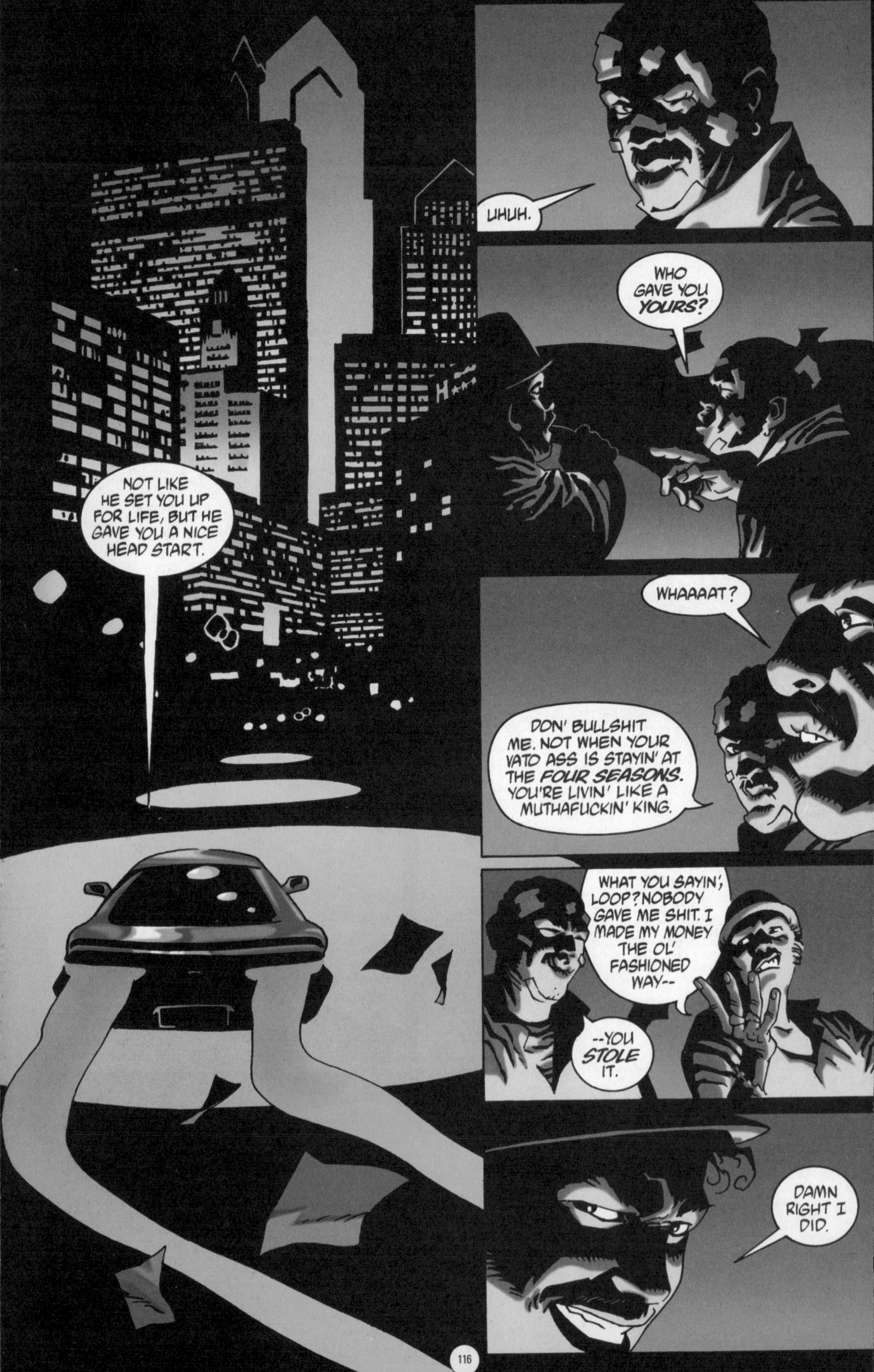
UHUH.
WHO GAVE YOU YOURS?
NOT LIKE HE SET YOU UP FOR LIFE, BUT HE GAVE YOU A NICE HEAD START.
WHAAAAT?
DON' BULLSHIT ME. NOT WHEN YOUR VATO ASS IS STAYIN' AT THE FOUR SEASONS. YOU'RE LIVIN' LIKE A MUTHAFUCKIN' KING.
WHAT YOU SAYIN', LOOP? NOBODY GAVE ME SHIT. I MADE MY MONEY THE OL' FASHIONED WAY--
--YOU STOLE IT.
DAMN RIGHT I DID.

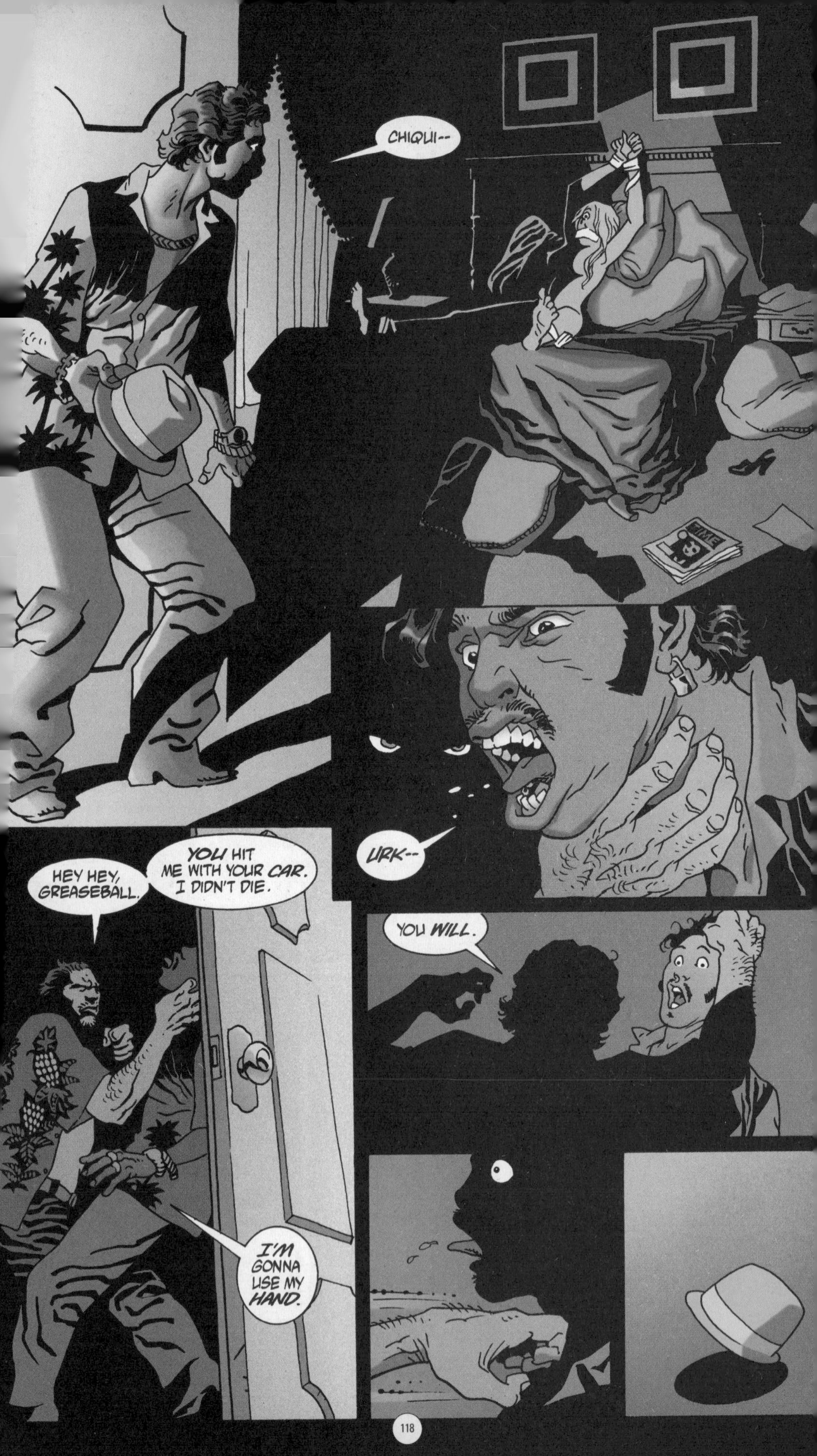

CHIQUI--
URK--
HEY HEY, GREASEBALL.
YOU HIT ME WITH YOUR CAR. I DIDN'T DIE.
I'M GONNA USE MY HAND.
YOU WILL.

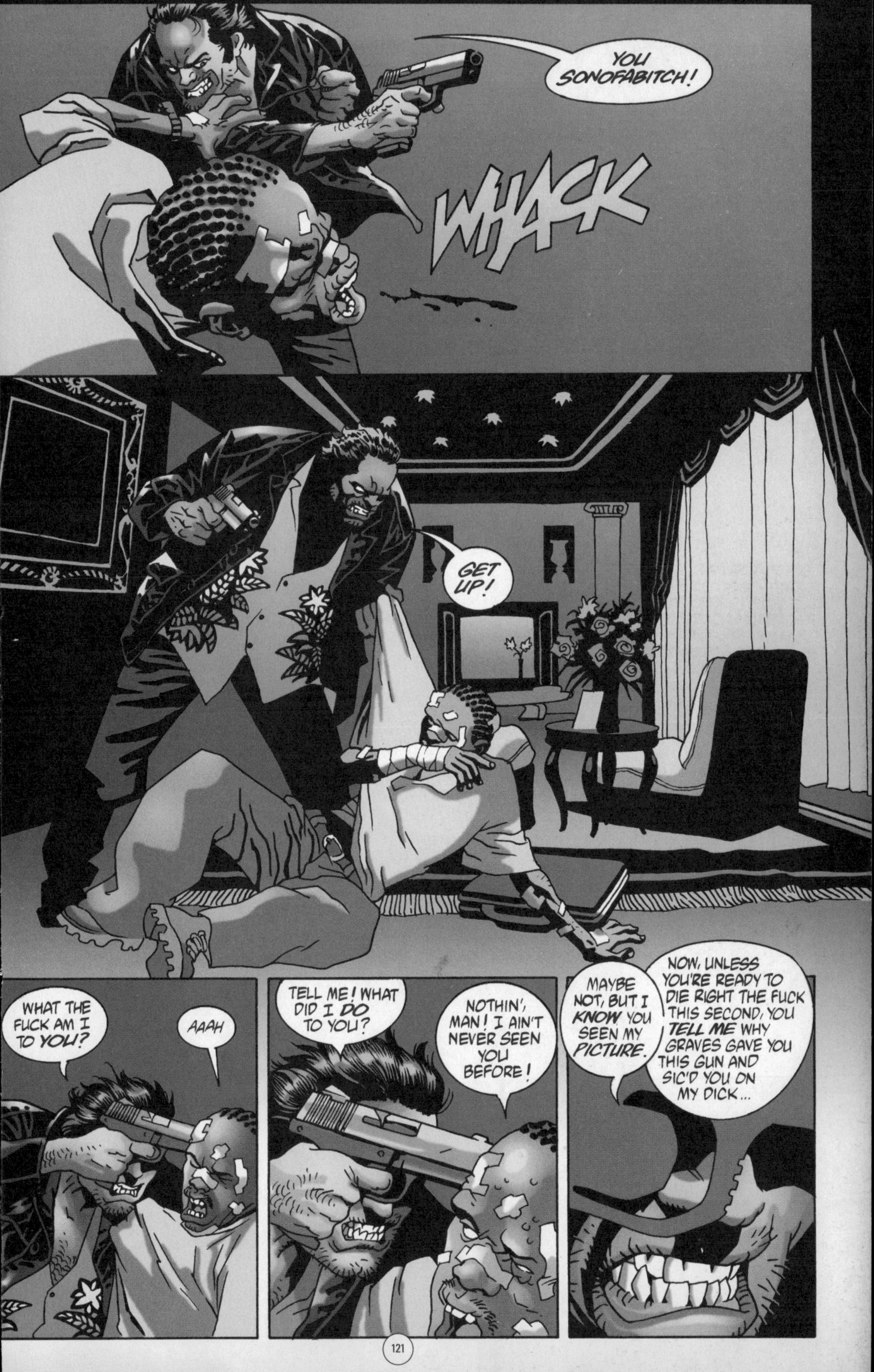
YOU SONOFABITCH!
WHACK
GET UP!
WHAT THE FUCK AM I TO YOU?
AAAH
TELL ME! WHAT DID I DO TO YOU?
NOTHIN', MAN! I AIN'T NEVER SEEN YOU BEFORE!
MAYBE NOT, BUT I KNOW YOU SEEN MY PICTURE.
NOW, UNLESS YOU'RE READY TO DIE RIGHT THE FUCK THIS SECOND, YOU TELL ME WHY GRAVES GAVE YOU THIS GUN AND SIC'D YOU ON MY DICK...

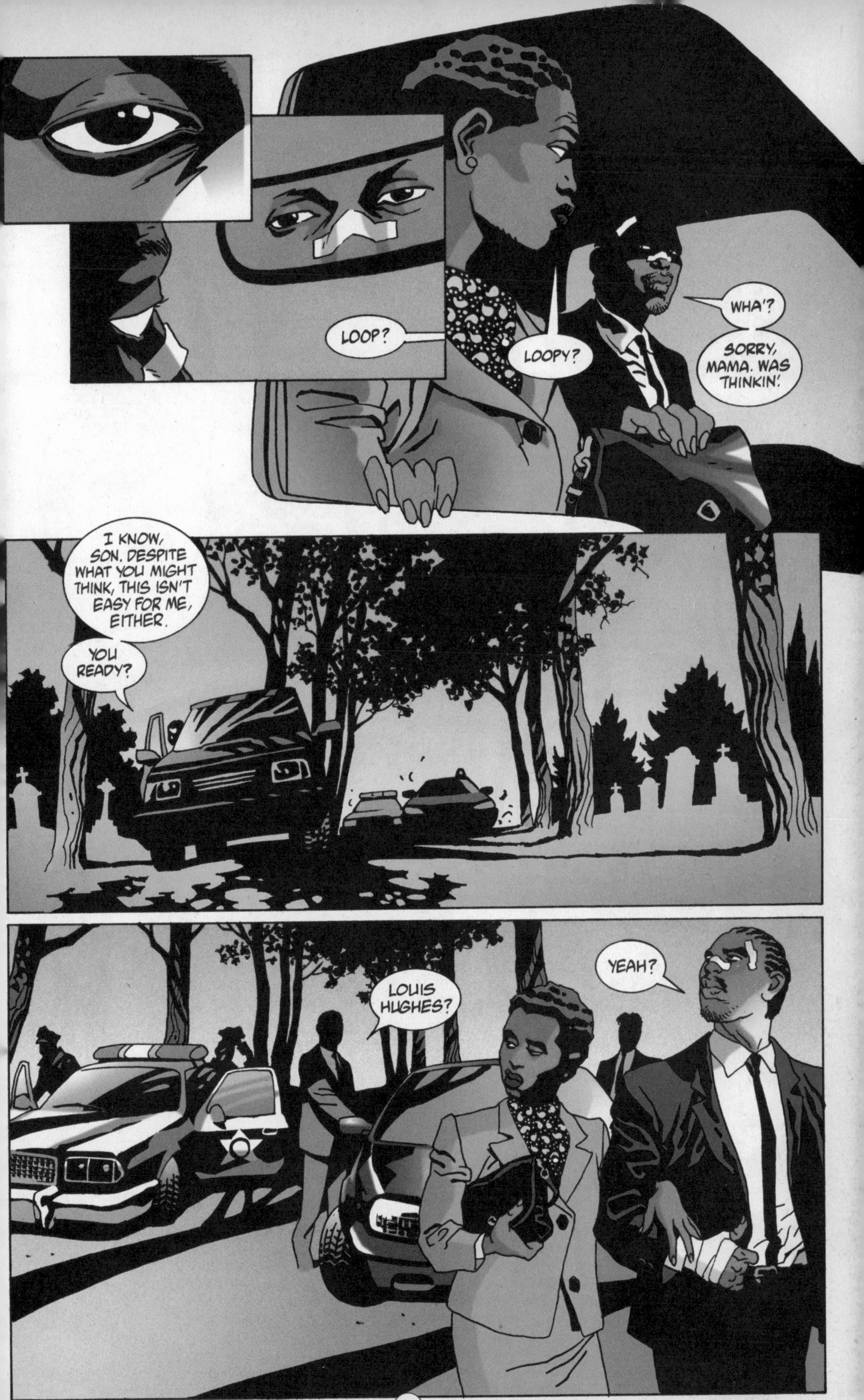
LOOP?
LOOPY?
WHA'?
SORRY, MAMA. WAS THINKIN'.
I KNOW, SON. DESPITE WHAT YOU MIGHT THINK, THIS ISN'T EASY FOR ME, EITHER.
YOU READY?
LOUIS HUGHES?
YEAH?